D1207988

Religion in Nineteenth Century America

Religion in American Life

JON BUTLER & HARRY S. STOUT
GENERAL EDITORS

Religion in Nineteenth Century America

Grant Wacker

OXFORD UNIVERSITY PRESS
New York • Oxford

For Julia, who turned ideals into deeds
Americorps City Year, San Jose 1998–99

Oxford University Press

Oxford New York
Athens Auckland Bangkok Bogotá Buenos Aires Calcutta
Cape Town Chennai Dar es Salaam Delhi Florence Hong Kong Istanbul
Karachi Kuala Lumpur Madrid Melbourne Mexico City Mumbai
Nairobi Paris São Paulo Singapore Taipei Tokyo Toronto Warsaw
and associated companies in
Berlin Ibadan

Published by Oxford University Press, Inc.
198 Madison Avenue, New York, New York 10016
www.oup.com

Oxford is a registered trademark of Oxford University Press

Library of Congress Cataloging-in-Publication Data

Wacker, Grant.
Religion in 19th century America/by Grant Wacker
p. cm. — (Religion in American life)
Includes bibliographic references and index.
Summary: Tours the ever-shifting landscape of 19th-century America,
reflecting the constant change of religious life in that century.
ISBN 0-19-511021-8 (alk. Paper)
1. United States—Religion—19th century—Juvenile literature.
2. United States—Church history—19th century—Juvenile literature.
[1. United States—Church history—19th century.] I. Title. II. Series.
BL2525.W33 2000   200'.973'09034—dc21   99-088938

ISBN 0-19-511021-8 (library edition)

9 8 7 6 5 4 3 2 1

Printed in the United States of America
on acid-free paper

Design and layout: Loraine Machlin
Picture research: Lisa Kirchner

On the cover: Vespers by Gari Julius Melchers

Frontispiece: Presbyterian Mission School employees and their children
head home after Sunday church in Oklahoma.

Contents

Editors' Introduction

JON BUTLER & HARRY S. STOUT, GENERAL EDITORS

History, as every historian knows, is about change over time. Anthropologists look at "culture," and sociologists analyze "society," but only historians tell stories that trace people and events over many generations. Thus it is important that this series examine not only individual religious groups, but also the interactions of these groups over three long periods of time: the colonial era, the 19th century, and the 20th century.

In this volume Grant Wacker traces the middle period of America's religious past. He begins with the American Revolution and its novel separation of church and state. Nobody knew where this great experiment in religious liberty would lead. In this book we see how Americans of diverse religious traditions and heritages made their peace with, and even thrived in, the new republic. Along the way we see entirely new religious traditions emerge, and new challenges, with the Civil War and the Industrial Revolution. This book is part of a unique 17-volume series that explores the evolution, character, and dynamics of religion in American life from 1500 to the end of the 20th century. As late as the 1960s, historians paid relatively little attention to religion beyond studies of New England's Puritans. But since then, American religious history and its contemporary expression have been the subject of intense inquiry. These new studies have thoroughly transformed our knowledge of almost every American religious group and have fully revised our understanding of religion's role in U.S. history.

It is impossible to capture the flavor and character of the American experience without understanding the connections between secular activities and religion. Spirituality stood at the center of Native American societies before European colonization and has continued to do so long after. Religion—and the freedom to express it—motivated millions of immigrants to come to the United States from remarkably different cultures, and the exposure to new ideas and ways of living shaped their experience. It also fueled tension among different ethnic and racial groups in the United States and, regretfully, accounted for difficult episodes of bigotry in American society. Religion urged Americans to expand the nation—first within the continental United States, then through overseas conquests and missionary work—and has had a profound influence on American politics, from the era of the Puritans to the present. Finally, religion contributes to the extraordinary diversity that has, for four centuries, made the United States one of the world's most dynamic societies.

The Religion in American Life series explores the historical traditions that have made religious freedom and spiritual exploration central features of American society. It emphasizes the experience of religion in America—what men and women have understood by religion, how it has affected politics and society, and how Americans have used it to shape their daily lives.

Religion in American Life

JON BUTLER & HARRY S. STOUT
GENERAL EDITORS

RELIGION IN COLONIAL AMERICA
Jon Butler

RELIGION IN NINETEENTH CENTURY AMERICA
Grant Wacker

RELIGION IN TWENTIETH CENTURY AMERICA
Randall Balmer

BUDDHISTS, HINDUS, AND SIKHS IN AMERICA
Gurinder Singh Mann, Paul David Numrich, & Raymond B. Williams

CATHOLICS IN AMERICA
James T. Fisher

JEWS IN AMERICA
Hasia R. Diner

MORMONS IN AMERICA
Claudia Lauper Bushman & Richard Lyman Bushman

MUSLIMS IN AMERICA
Frederick Denny

ORTHODOX CHRISTIANS IN AMERICA
John A. Erickson

PROTESTANTS IN AMERICA
Mark Noll

AFRICAN-AMERICAN RELIGION
Albert J. Raboteau

ALTERNATIVE AMERICAN RELIGIONS
Stephen J. Stein

CHURCH AND STATE IN AMERICA
Edwin S. Gaustad

IMMIGRATION AND AMERICAN RELIGION
Jenna Weissman Joselit

NATIVE AMERICAN RELIGION
Joel W. Martin

WOMEN AND AMERICAN RELIGION
Ann Braude

BIOGRAPHICAL SUPPLEMENT AND SERIES INDEX
Darryl Hart & Ann Henderson Hart

Preface

"There is no country in the world where the Christian religion
retains a greater influence over the souls of men than in America."

These words flowed from the pen of Alexis de Tocqueville, a French traveler visiting the United States in 1831. De Tocqueville was not the only European visitor impressed by the vitality of religion in the new land. Nearly 60 years later, an English traveler named James Bryce remarked that churches seemed to pop up everywhere, and everywhere equally. "Possibly half of the native population go to church at least once every Sunday," he judged, thoroughly amazed. Shortly afterward, Francis Grund, a Czech visitor, left with similar feelings: "The religious habits of Americans form not only the basis of their private and public morals but have become . . . thoroughly interwoven with . . . the very essence of their government." Some European guests thought that American religion was rather disorderly, but none doubted its diversity or its explosive energy.

This book provides an overview of the ever-shifting religious landscape of the United States in the 19th century. The journey will actually begin slightly earlier, just after the American Revolution, in the 1780s, when the founders established patterns that would linger through the 19th century and into the present. From time to time we shall look beyond the 19th century into the 20th, in order to learn how certain stories turned out. But we shall mainly focus upon the luxuriant growth of U.S. religious groups in the dozen decades stretching from the formation of the young republic to the opening of the modern era.

Along the way, watch for three long-range trends. The first is the enduring power of evangelical Protestants, in denominations such as Methodist, Baptist, and Presbyterian. For most of the century these groups, taken together, ran the biggest, wealthiest, and most influential organized-religion show in town. But they never ran the only show.

Their competition constitutes the second trend. Throughout the century, evangelical Protestants saw constant, intense contention from rival groups, including non-evangelical Protestants, Roman Catholics, Jews, and others who refused to bow to the majority.

The third long-range trend is the continual churning among the denominations. Those that enjoyed dominance in one generation often found themselves playing catch-up in the next. As an example of how things can change, in 1800 the Congregationalists (once the Puritans) led the pack. They then claimed nearly a fifth of all Christians in this country. The Presbyterians and Baptists ran a close second and third, followed by the Episcopalians. Trailing far behind were the Methodists and the Roman Catholics.

By the middle of the century, however, this ranking had been turned virtually upside down. By then the Roman Catholics and Methodists were wrestling for first place. The Baptists were still third, but now they were followed by the Presbyterians, the Congregationalists, and an entirely new group, the Christian Church/Disciples of Christ. In 1900 things looked completely different again. At that point the Catholics were on top, followed by the Baptists, Methodists, and, newcomers to the top four, the Lutherans. Pentecostals, who would loom large at the end of the 20th century, were just around the corner.

Throughout this book I have tried to write from the perspective of the historical actors themselves. I have endeavored to describe the world as they saw and interpreted it. If they said that they received a revelation from God, or felt oppressed by a dominant majority, I have taken them at their word. This does not mean that the readers of these statements should suspend their judgment of them. But it does mean that our first task, as students of U.S. religious history, is to raise the dead and let them speak for themselves. That said, the journey beckons.

Chapter 1

Founders

My country, tis of thee, sweet land of
liberty, of thee I sing; land where my
fathers died, land of the pilgrims pride,
from every mountainside let freedom ring!
  —*Samuel F. Smith, "America" (1832)*

Things looked grim. When the guns at the Yorktown, Virginia, battlefield
fell silent in the fall of 1781, ending the Revolutionary War, the young
nation found itself in disarray, as did its churches. At most, one person in
10, and perhaps only one in 20, counted themselves a member of any
organized religious body. Many ministers had abandoned their pulpits,
either to serve as chaplains or to fight the enemy. Sometimes they battled
as Tories, loyal to the British crown, sometimes as patriots, and sometimes
they refused to fight for either side, an independence for which they paid
dearly. Revival meetings designed to rekindle religious zeal had flourished
off and on for the better part of 50 years. Yet those too finally sputtered.
For the past decade, people had been preoccupied first with political matters and then with the war for independence. Apathy reigned.

At the beginning of the war, many patriots believed that Christ himself would return to earth, first to defeat the British redcoats, and then to
establish his reign of peace and righteousness for a thousand years. But
now, with that hope dashed, what remained?

Things looked darker for some groups than for others. The Church
of England, which had dominated the southern colonies and remained

Chaplain Jacob Duché leads
the first prayer offered in
Congress on September 7,
1774, in Philadelphia.
Though the new country's
leaders did not want the
government to support religion in official ways, after
the federal government
was set up in 1789, religious
services were often held in
federal buildings.

strong in the urban centers of the North, now faced the crisis of its life. Virtually all of its clergy outside New England had fled the country. Those who remained were now required by their vows to swear allegiance to the king. But how could they do so, since the colonies had just revolted from England and proclaimed themselves an independent nation? The Church of England eventually solved this problem by reorganizing itself in 1789 as the Protestant Episcopal Church in the U.S.A. But it would be many decades until that body would achieve the kind of strength and stability it had enjoyed before the Revolution.

The Methodists too faced hard times. They had started in England in the 1730s as a reform movement within the Church of England. Methodist preachers came to the colonies in the 1760s. There they tried to build their followers' enthusiasm in Church of England gatherings, just as they had done at home. But their founder, John Wesley, had strongly opposed the Revolution, making Methodist sympathizers in the colonies suspect at best. All but one of Mr. Wesley's preachers, as they were called, returned to England during the war.

Thus, after the Revolution the Methodists in the United States too faced a major decision. Should they just let their movement die? Ought they to try to carry on as a revival impulse in the crippled Church of England in America? Or should they form their own sect (upstart group)? The denomination's leaders, meeting in Baltimore on a wintry Christmas Eve in 1784, decided to embrace the last option: to form their own sect. The infant denomination, which they called the Methodist Episcopal Church, grew rapidly. Indeed, for most of the following century the new sect would rank as the largest Protestant body in the nation.

Most of the other major religious groups in the colonies also had to struggle to get back on their feet. The Congregationalists (or Puritans) and the Presbyterians did best, partly because they had supported the winning side during the Revolution. The Lutherans experienced more problems, for precisely the opposite reason: many had failed to support the patriots. And the Quakers, once very strong, faced even more severe problems. As pacifists, most had refused to fight at all. Many Americans doubted the Quakers' loyalty to the new nation and shunned them.

Altogether, then, great stretches of the religious landscape looked bleak: meeting houses destroyed, people apathetic, ministers gone, long-established denominations in disarray. The churches all found themselves wondering how to reorganize in the face of a new nation with new laws and new expectations.

But appearances proved to be deceiving. In fact, many found the prospects exhilarating. In 1782, for example, J. Hector St. Jean de Crève-coeur, a French farmer in upstate New York, declared that the new land contained the embryos of all the arts, sciences, and ingenuity that flour-ished in Europe. In America one beheld "fair cities, substantial villages, extensive fields, an immense country filled with decent houses, good roads, orchards, meadows, and bridges, where an hundred years ago all was wild, woody and uncultivated!" This vision proved intoxicating:

This 1787 painting by Edward Hicks of David Twining's prosperous farm captures the idealism expressed in J. Hector St. John de Crèvecoeur's *Letters from an American Farmer*. Religious freedom was an important part of Crèvecoeur's dream.

"[We] are the most perfect society now existing in the world." De Crève-coeur summed up his feelings in words that would be quoted repeatedly by subsequent generations:

> The American is a new man, who acts upon new principles; he must therefore entertain new ideas, and form new opinions. From involuntary idleness, servile dependence, penury, and useless labour, he has passed to toils of a very different nature. . . . This is an American.

This appreciative Frenchman perceived, albeit dimly, that the young nation was beginning to forge a dramatically new way to organize religion as part of its new independent identity. Today we take for granted that people may worship any time and anywhere they want as long as they do not disturb their neighbors. Or they may not worship at all, if they prefer. We also take for granted that the government will not help religious groups in any systematic or significant way, except for incidental help, such as, for instance, in putting out a fire. But in the 1780s and 1790s religious liberty and the separation of church and state were largely new ideas in the Western world. How did this immense change come about?

Most of the colonies assumed that everyone living in a given colony should belong to the same religious tradition. They also assumed that this tradition should receive support from the state, either through tax money or through laws forcing people to attend the primary church, or both. This arrangement was called the established religion. Even Pennsylvania and Maryland, two colonies that had allowed substantial religious freedom in the beginning, presented a mixed record regarding religious tolerance. At one time or another Roman Catholics found themselves barred from public office in both places.

By the time of the Revolution the idea of having one established religion had come under sharp criticism. Thoughtful men and women raised three arguments against it. Thomas Jefferson, author of the Declaration of Independence, governor of Virginia, and the third President of the United States, offered the first one. Jefferson insisted that people should be free to choose their own religion, or no religion at all, just as they should be free to choose where they lived or what kind of job they held.

Thomas Jefferson Writes of the Freedom to Choose

Thomas Jefferson, the third President of the United States, believed that men and women should be free to select their religious beliefs without interference, let alone coercion, from the government. He made this point often, but nowhere more forcefully than in his only book, Notes on the State of Virginia *(1785).*

The legitimate powers of government extend to such acts only as are injurious to others. But it does me no injury to say that there are twenty gods, or no God. It neither picks my pocket nor breaks my leg. . . . Reason and free inquiry are the only effectual agents against error. . . . It is error alone which needs the support of government. Truth can stand by itself. . . . [Is] uniformity of opinion desirable? No more than of face and stature. . . . Is uniformity attainable? Millions of innocent men, women, and children, since the introduction of Christianity, have been burnt, tortured, fined, imprisoned; yet we have not advanced one inch towards uniformity. What has been the effect of coercion? To make one half the world fools, the other half hypocrites. . . . Reason and persuasion are the only practicable instruments. To make way for these, free inquiry must be indulged; and how can we wish others to indulge it while we refuse it ourselves[?]

Freedom of religion was a natural right, he argued, one that people held simply because they were human. Besides, Jefferson added, what people imagine to be true about God does no harm one way or another. "[I]t does me no injury for my neighbor to say there are twenty gods, or no god. It neither picks my pocket nor breaks my leg." Coercion by the state in matters of religion simply did not work, he said. The result was "to make one half the world fools, the other half hypocrites."

The second argument against established religion found a strong voice in Isaac Backus, a Baptist pastor in Massachusetts in the Revolutionary era. Backus believed that it was not fair for the government to support one religious group but not others. It was not the government's job to decide which one was right, he argued. And supporting all the different religious groups would not solve the problem either. Backus worried that state support for religion would do more harm than good. When Christians (or anyone else, for that matter) took money from the state for the support of their churches, sooner or later they would have to pay the price.

To be sure, the Baptists worried about the prevalence of "Gaming, Dancing, and Sabbath-Day Diversions," as one of their opponents put it. But the Baptists felt that government coercion offered no solution. Backus himself paid a steep price for his views. The authorities repeatedly fined and jailed him for refusing to pay taxes that would go to the support of a rival group. But Backus's ideas gradually won wide respect. Later generations would regard him as a lonely pioneer of the Baptist conscience in America.

James Madison voiced the third argument against establishment. Madison followed Thomas Jefferson as President. Though only a wisp of a man and constantly worried about his health, Madison exerted immense influence upon American religion. He believed that the young nation had become too diverse for the government to support one religion over another. Things might be different if everyone held the same views, he supposed, but in fact they did not. The young republic harbored dozens of competing sects, each jostling the others for a place in the new American sun. Madison's position might be called the practical argument against established religion: it just did not work.

In the 1780s these three reasons for opposing a religious establishment—reasons based on principle, on conscience, and on practicality—flowed together and informed the writing of the Constitution and the First Amendment. (Madison served as the main author of both.) Article VI of the Constitution states that "no religious Test shall ever be required as a Qualification to any Office of public Trust under the United States." The Constitution does not mention God or say anything else directly about religion, thus making it one of the most secular (nonreligious) documents of the modern world.

Madison and the other signers of the Constitution did not mean to say that religion was unimportant. What they sought was to remove religion

At least 1,500 citizens signed *A Memorial and Remonstrance,* James Madison's petition for religious liberty, before it was submitted to the October 1785 session of the Virginia Assembly. This meticulously hand-written copy may have been Madison's personal keepsake.

from national politics. They tried to say, in other words, that religion was one thing, politics another, and people should not mix them up. The First Amendment to the Constitution, ratified in 1791, contained the following words about the federal government's relation to religion: "Congress shall make no law respecting an establishment of religion, or prohibiting the free exercise thereof." This sentence aimed to reinforce the main point of Article VI in the Constitution: that government should stay out of the religion business, neither helping nor harming the religious institutions of the land.

But there was more to the story. Although the founders did not want the federal government to help religion in formal or official ways, they had no qualms about its rendering incidental assistance, and they certainly saw no reason that government officials should hide their personal commitments. President George Washington, for example, set aside November 26, 1789, as a national day of prayer, repentance, and Thanksgiving to God. John Adams, the second President, continued Washington's prayer day tradition. Adams boldly called himself a "church-going animal," and in his inaugural address specified a "decent respect for Christianity" as a recommendation for public service.

Jefferson, the third President, not only attended church regularly while President but also generously supported the construction of meetinghouses of various sects in the Washington area. For more than a half century, from 1800 through the 1860s, believers regularly used the House of Representatives for worship. Episcopalians, Congregationalists, Baptists, Methodists, Quakers, Unitarians, and even Catholics each had their turn. Throughout the period, other federal buildings also saw use for worship, including the sacrament of Holy Communion and old-fashioned revival services.

The Constitution and the First Amendment applied only to the federal government, however, leaving the states free to do as they wished regarding the establishment of religion. Some people worried that the federal government might be making a terrible mistake. Connecticut, New Hampshire, and Massachusetts thus continued to support the Congregational church with tax money for many years: Connecticut until

1818, New Hampshire until the following year, and Massachusetts until 1833. Patrick Henry, the Revolutionary War orator who won lasting fame for his "Give me liberty or give me death" speech, wanted his beloved Virginia to continue to support all religions equally. South Carolina even wrote that aim into its constitution.

But most Americans disagreed. Virginia, the home of Jefferson and Madison, moved swiftly to eliminate state support for religion, abolishing taxes for the livelihood of the clergy in 1776 and guaranteeing religious freedom for everyone nine years later. Sooner or later most of the other states followed Virginia's path, sometimes grudgingly, at other times eagerly. The invigorating breeze of political liberty inspired them to desire religious liberty as well.

The closing years of the 18th century saw the birth of another pattern that remains strong today. That trend went by various names. Some philosophers called it political religion. Benjamin Franklin dubbed it "Publick Religion." After World War II many called it civil religion. By whatever name, political or public or civil religion stemmed from a desire to give religious meaning to the nation itself. It represented more than patriotism or love of country. Rather it symbolized a desire to place the United States in a larger framework of significance, an attempt to say that America occupied a special or even unique place in God's plan for the world. In civil religion, in other words, religious language blurred with political language so that the two became almost indistinguishable.

Even today, civil religion hangs in the atmosphere like a fine mist. We pledge allegiance to the flag (a political statement) but, in the same breath, go on to say that the nation stands "under God" (a religious statement). Memorial Day and the Fourth of July are more than political celebrations. They prompt bowed heads and moist eyes as flags flutter over courthouses and churches alike. Each year thousands of tourists file past the looming statue of Abraham Lincoln at his memorial in Washington, D.C. They whisper, with caps removed, as if they were in a cathedral. We treat some political figures, especially in death, as if they were saints. Abraham Lincoln and John F. Kennedy come to mind. At the same time, we permit some religious figures to speak about political matters with the authority

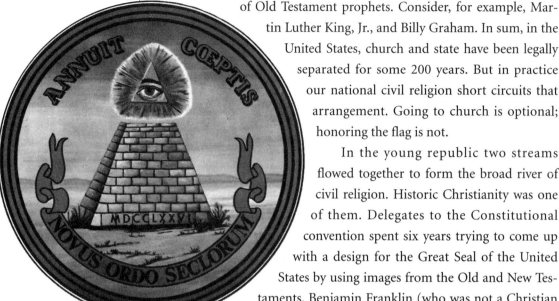

Much of the six-year debate over the design of the Great Seal of the United States focused on religious imagery. The committee settled on the eye and the motto *Annuit Coeptis* (He [God] has ordered our way) on the reverse side of the seal to symbolize the moral and religious right of the American cause.

of Old Testament prophets. Consider, for example, Martin Luther King, Jr., and Billy Graham. In sum, in the United States, church and state have been legally separated for some 200 years. But in practice our national civil religion short circuits that arrangement. Going to church is optional; honoring the flag is not.

In the young republic two streams flowed together to form the broad river of civil religion. Historic Christianity was one of them. Delegates to the Constitutional convention spent six years trying to come up with a design for the Great Seal of the United States by using images from the Old and New Testaments. Benjamin Franklin (who was not a Christian by any conventional definition of the term) wanted the seal to depict Moses dividing the Red Sea. Jefferson wanted it to show the Israelites trekking through the wilderness.

The other stream of the religious tradition was the religions and cultures of ancient Greece and Rome. The architectural style of Greek and Roman temples turned up everywhere in the new republic, especially in the bustling new town of Washington, D.C. Thus John Adams wanted the Great Seal to bear a Roman image of the god Hercules torn between Virtue (pointing upward) and Sloth (aimed downward).

The design on an early dollar bill offered a clear example of the way that Christian and classical (Greek and Roman) themes entwined. One side of the design displayed a pyramid with an eye at the top. Latin inscriptions stood above and below the pyramid. One said "Annuit Coeptis" (He has ordered our way): in other words, God Himself would guide the new nation. The other read "Novus Ordo Seclorum" (New order of the ages): in other words, the young republic would mark the beginning of a fresh age of human history. This hope stemmed from the New Testament Book of Revelation, but also from the Greek and Roman notion that history ran in cycles. Thus, the American experiment represented the rebirth of the beauty and advanced civilization of ancient Greece and Rome.

The twisting of Christian and classical strands found its clearest expression in the veneration bestowed upon President George Washington. During his lifetime people clamored for locks of his hair, named babies after him, and spoke of his uncanny abilities as a military general. In 1779, 20 years before his death, a Pennsylvania German-language almanac called him the father of the country. People duly noted that Washington's mother was named Mary and his wife Martha. Could these names, which loomed large in the New Testament stories about Jesus, be a mere coincidence? Americans likened him to Moses, who had freed the Israelites from slavery, and to Joshua, who had fought bravely for the Lord. At the same time, they also compared Washington to the Roman military general Cincinnatus, who preferred farming to fighting. After the President's death, people solemnly noted that an eagle, the national bird, had

An 1846 daguerreotype of the Capitol building shows the architectural style inspired by classical temples—a reference to the advanced civilizations of ancient Greece and Rome and the hope that the young country would begin a new, equally powerful era in history.

flown over his tomb. And when Washington's body was moved in 1837 to a new marble coffin, reports said that the body showed almost no decay.

The theory and practice of civil religion waxed and waned throughout the 19th century. It proved to be particularly conspicuous in times of war or national stress when the people needed assurance that their nation was favored by the Almighty. The esteem bestowed upon the fallen—some said martyred—President Lincoln in 1865 rivaled the attention given Washington and many of the saints of the church. It was no accident that some of the songs Americans came to love best—"America," "The Battle Hymn of the Republic," and "America the Beautiful"—mixed religious and patriotic themes line by line. (Indeed, Samuel F. Smith, a Baptist pastor in New England, penned the first in 1832, Julia Ward Howe, a Unitarian activist and abolitionist, dashed off the second in 1861, and Katherine Lee Bates, daughter of a Congregationalist minister, wrote the last in 1904.)

After the Revolution many Americans not only embraced civil religion but also resisted traditional forms of authority, especially the oppressive weight of historic Christianity. Today television evangelists commonly talk about the deep Christian faith of the founding fathers. In truth, most of those preachers would almost certainly be horrified if any of the first four Presidents of the United States—Washington, Adams, Jefferson, or Madison—turned up in their congregations and said what they really thought about Christianity. All were courageous and high-minded men, but none was a Christian in any conventional way.

Consider George Washington. The first President believed in a creator God, held the Bible in high esteem, and respected the teachings of Jesus. He served as a leader in his local Episcopal church and went out of his way to show respect for Christianity in public. When he first took the oath of office, for example, he laid his hand on a Bible and added "So help me God," a practice followed by all subsequent Presidents. But Washington always referred to God in distant, impersonal terms such as Providence, Almighty Being, Great Author, or Invisible Hand. He worshiped irregularly, rarely took Holy Communion, refused to kneel to pray, and regarded Jesus as a fine man but did not consider him divine.

Even during his lifetime, George Washington was seen as an almost divine figure. Sitting on a cloud with an arm outstretched and an angel placing a halo-like wreath on his head, Washington is clearly an icon of Christian worship in this early American painting.

Privately, Washington probably remained skeptical about the main doctrines of Christianity.

Thomas Jefferson proved to be even more radical about religion than Washington. Like Washington, Jefferson believed that a supreme God existed and that Jesus' ethical teachings offered useful guidelines for daily life. He never disparaged religion in public. Jefferson defended the doctrine of the strict separation of church and state because that arrangement allowed citizens to worship or not worship as they pleased. But his God

Thomas Jefferson was a staunch supporter of religious freedom. "The constitutional freedom of religion [is] the most inalienable and sacred of all human rights," Jefferson stated to the Virginia Board of Visitors in 1819.

was tangible, like the deities of pagan Greece and Rome. The miracles attributed to Jesus struck Jefferson as so absurd that he went to the trouble of putting together his own version of the New Testament, popularly called the Jefferson Bible, with all the supernatural elements scissored out. The Virginian's strongest grievance, however, was not against Christian doctrine but against Christian priests and ministers. He felt that they persuaded people to "give up morals for mysteries" and that they took advantage of people by cheating them of their hard-earned dollars.

The ideas of individuals like Washington and Jefferson often received the label Deism, which might be defined as the belief that God created but did not involve himself in the world thereafter. How common was Deism? The short answer is, not very. In matters of religion the founders spoke for an influential and well-educated elite, but not many others. Even so, they merit study, since they shaped the church–state patterns of the young republic. Those patterns persist today remarkably intact.

At the beginning of the 19th century another group of antitraditionalists won more support, especially among the college educated and the rising middle class. They called themselves Unitarians. The creed of the Unitarians, outsiders quipped, affirmed the fatherhood of God, the brotherhood of man, and the neighborhood of Boston. The quip held considerable truth, for the Unitarians did believe in God's essential unity. For them, Jesus Christ ranked high as a uniquely moral man, possibly even divine in some sense, but not equal to God the father. The Holy Spirit referred not to the third person of the Trinity but to God's actions in history.

Unitarians also thought that humans, who were born without original sin, could learn to live productive lives through education. With effort and foresight human history could become a story of moral progress rather than an unending cycle of war and suffering. As for Boston, most Unitarians did in fact live in New England, and many attended or taught at Harvard, but their ideas extended far and wide. Unitarian ideas powerfully stirred 19th-century writers such as Henry David Thoreau (author of *Walden*) and Ralph Waldo Emerson (who wrote *Nature*), as well as reformers like Dorothea Dix (who helped establish asylums for the insane) and Julia Ward Howe (who fought slavery).

Other Americans forged their own nontraditional paths to religious truth. The Secret Society of Freemasons, commonly known as the Freemasons, or just Masons, provided one of the most common options. The Masons traced their origin to ancient Egypt, symbolized by the pyramid on the dollar bill. That notion reflected mostly wishful thinking, but it offered the security of connecting Americans with a source of wisdom in the distant past. The Masons actually started in England in the 12th century as an all-male fraternity of craftsmen. The first Masonic lodge in the colonies opened in Philadelphia in 1731. Rapid growth followed. Almost all the signers of the Declaration of Independence were Masons, as were many members of the Continental Congress.

Masonry (and hundreds of similar orders, such as the Odd Fellows, Knights of Pythias, and Prince Hall Masons) flourished in the 19th century, among blacks as well as whites. They offered men a form of fellowship different from ordinary religion, one rich with rituals, special clothes, and secret passwords. The Masons emphasized brotherhood and fair dealing. While some embraced Christianity, many others felt that people should outgrow that religion in favor of a more rational and useful one like theirs. The Masons saw God as a grand architect who designed the universe according to natural law. Their symbols centered upon the carpenter's square and the compass, building tools that suggested firmness of character (square dealing) and high ideals (aiming high, as the compass pointed toward the sky). Just as the sun provided light for the physical universe, reason, the internal sun, supplied light to the human universe. Thus the eternal eye of God, symbolizing reason, peered from the top of the pyramid on the dollar bill.

This "emblematic chart" is filled with the symbols and history of the Freemasons, including an all-seeing eye, beehive, lamb, and anchor. Many of the Masonic religious rituals have been kept secret for centuries.

Many citizens of the new republic who resisted traditional Christianity still considered themselves Christians. Jefferson, for example, called himself a Christian to the end. Many Masons attended their own lodge meetings on Saturday, then church on Sunday. Beyond these patterns, thousands of rank-and-file Christians perpetuated the religious practices of their ancestors. They used divining rods to find water, amulets to ward off evil spirits, and special potions to stir affection in the opposite sex. They consulted the stars to learn their future. They sought to heal through the use of white magic and to curse through the use of black magic (terms that may have held racial overtones). Some clergymen worried about all this mixing and matching, but most ordinary people thought nothing of it.

Most importantly, as the 18th century slipped into the 19th, thousands of Americans drifted away from traditional Christianity simply because it no longer met their needs. In the minds of many, the two largest and strongest groups before the Revolution, the Congregationalists (the Puritans) and the Church of England (the Anglicans) left much to be desired. The former seemed to overstress God's arbitrariness and the importance of a well-educated clergy. The latter seemed to overemphasize hierarchies, creeds, and liturgies.

But did that kind of religion—starchy and intellectual—represent the true message of the New Testament? Or was God's grace available to any who asked for it? Could ordinary people read the Bible for themselves and decide what it meant? Should not worship lead to heartfelt conversion and a morally rigorous life? Millions who answered these questions affirmatively drifted from the older groups. They joined new ones—new in the United States, anyway—that called themselves Baptists and Methodists and Disciples of Christ. By the opening of the Civil War, the upstarts had come to reign as the new religious insiders.

Chapter 2

Insiders

Just as I am, without one plea,
but that thy blood was shed for me,
and that thou bidst me come to thee,
O Lamb of God, I come, I come.
　　—*Charlotte Elliott, "Just as I Am, Without One Plea" (1835)*

John Hagerty, a Baltimore Methodist preacher, published this Tree of Life in 1791. The 12 fruits of salvation, esteemed by evangelicals everywhere, hung on the tree and suggested the condemnation of the smug sinners below.

The first half of the 19th century witnessed the dramatic expansion of a religious movement that had started a hundred years earlier in England and Scotland. Its supporters called it evangelicalism. The word *evangelical* came into the English language from Greek and Latin terms that meant messenger of good news, or gospel. And good news it was. Evangelists spread the word that Christ's death and resurrection had freed sinners from their shackles and reconciled them to God. They preached this message in meetings called revivals, where they proclaimed that believers' flagging faith could be revived to vigorous new life. The evangelical stirring would rank as the largest, strongest, most sustained religious movement in U.S. history.

In America revivals began in a serious way with the preaching of English itinerant George Whitefield in the 1730s and 1740s. Commonly called the Great Awakening, these revivals sputtered out during and after the Revolutionary War years, but then reappeared at the end of the century and persisted off and on through the 1830s. They cropped up again

THE

SPIRITUAL SONGSTER:

CONTAINING A VARIETY OF

CAMP-MEETING,

AND OTHER

HYMNS.

Be glad in the Lord, and rejoice ye righteous, and shout for joy all ye that are upright in heart.—Ps. 32. v. 11.

FIRST EDITION.

PRINTED AND PUBLISHED BY GEORGE KOLB, FREDERICK-TOWN, MARYLAND. 1819.

Quick to recognize a market when they saw one, publishers produced cheap, handy songbooks for outdoor camp meetings. This 1819 hymnal brought joy to backwoods lives marked by toil and loneliness.

just before the Civil War and ran until its end in 1865. Later observers would call the entire era, running for the better part of 70 years, the Second Great Awakening (to distinguish it from the Great Awakening of the 1730s and 1740s). It would be inaccurate to suppose that everyone in antebellum (pre–Civil War) America considered themselves evangelicals, let alone supporters of revivals. But never again would a single religious outlook come so close to defining what it meant to be an insider in U.S. culture.

The Great Awakening and the Second Great Awakening bore important similarities, and one major difference. Both emphasized the authority of the Bible, a definable conversion experience based upon faith in Jesus Christ, and the importance of spreading the good news to others. But in the first Great Awakening men and women seemed to think and speak in the passive mood, as if to underscore God's action upon them. They saw themselves so hopelessly mired in sin that they could not even reach out to accept God's offer of grace. In dramatic contrast, the preachers of the Second Great Awakening routinely suggested that God had already given sinners the ability to accept grace when he offered it. It was up to them to take it or not. In the rough-and-tumble setting of 19th-century America, this message of human ability proved to be a spark in a powder keg.

The new revival began at roughly the same time, but in two different places. The first was in the Old Southwest, defined in those days as what is now Kentucky and Tennessee. Presbyterian pastor James McGready kindled the excitement. In 1797 McGready started praying fervently for the conversion of sinners in south-central Kentucky, where he lived. In the summer of 1800, scores of anxious men and women gathered outdoors to hear him speak. After four days of white-hot preaching, some of McGready's hearers nearly collapsed as they felt the weight of their sins. This pattern of coming together for days or even weeks for outdoor revivals—called camp meetings—resembled similar events that took place each fall in Scotland, but in the United States they proved to be more intense. One of the largest camp meetings in U.S. history soon followed. In August 1801 throngs of seekers gathered on a bluff called Cane Ridge, several miles northeast of Lexington. Estimates ranged from 10,000 to 25,000 souls. At the time Lexington itself numbered only 2,000 residents.

The Cane Ridge Revival, as it came to be known, is probably the most famous religious meeting in American history. Stirred by days of intense preaching, people responded with deep emotion. Observers noted that some worshipers wept uncontrollably while others appeared to laugh, twitch, and run in circles. Some even fell to their knees and barked like dogs. (At the time, outsiders called these actions "exercises." Today scholars call them trances, or involuntary motor behavior, a situation in which the brain loses control of the muscles under extreme stress.)

One observer described another outdoor meeting, also near Cane Ridge:

> Some [said] they feel the approaching symptoms by being under deep conviction; their heart swells, their nerves relax, and in an instant they become motionless and speechless. . . . It comes upon others like an electric shock, as if felt in the great arteries of the arms or thighs. . . . The body relaxes and falls motionless; the hands and feet become cold, and yet the pulse is as formerly. . . . They are all opposed to any medical application. . . . They will continue in that state from one hour to 24.

Soon hundreds of camp meetings of varying length and intensity erupted in the thinly settled territory beyond the Appalachians. Initially, well-schooled Presbyterians like McGready, as well as Baptist farmer-preachers and Methodist circuit riders, worked side by side to keep them going, but after a few years only Methodists participated. And by the

1820s even the Methodist camp meetings had toned down. After the Civil War, the Methodists set aside permanent sites—such as Round Lake in upstate New York, Martha's Vineyard in Massachusetts, and Ocean Grove in New Jersey—for annual religious encampments in pleasantly rustic settings. Although most people attended camp meetings primarily for religious reasons, many came for friendship and recreation as well.

The fires of the Second Great Awakening also burned brightly in the East, especially in the Congregational churches of southern New England. Yale College president Timothy Dwight took the lead. Dwight was no stranger to the revival tradition, for his grandfather, Jonathan Edwards, had led the first Great Awakening in Massachusetts. Dwight grieved deeply over the lack of faith among Yale's students. He was determined to stamp out infidelity through heartfelt preaching about the perils of

In extended outdoor revival meetings, fiery preachers stirred emotional responses among their hearers. Or was it the other way around? It is also possible that audiences, starved for fellowship (and entertainment), gave preachers their golden opportunity.

unbelief, and about Christ's love for wayward humans. The college president's fervor soon sparked revivals in local churches up and down the East Coast.

Others who promoted the revival in the churches of the East included two of Dwight's students, Lyman Beecher, the father of Harriet Beecher Stowe, author of *Uncle Tom's Cabin,* and Yale theologian Nathaniel W. Taylor. Bucking centuries of tradition, Beecher and Taylor suggested that human beings, though deeply sinful, nonetheless possessed the ability to accept God's grace, if they would only do so.

Then came two of the most energetic and gifted figures in the history of American religion: Francis Asbury and Charles Grandison Finney. The former labored almost everywhere except New England, the latter mostly in the urban centers of the northeast. Though Asbury was a Methodist and Finney a Presbyterian (later a Congregationalist), together they effectively defined the evangelical tradition in antebellum America.

THE PROPHET OF THE LONG ROAD

Francis Asbury ranked as the first and most famous of Methodist bishops. He drew on John Wesley's theology and Charles Wesley's hymns to form what became the largest Protestant denomination in the United States in the 19th century.

The new land to the west offered Asbury a majestic stage for displaying his evangelical talents. Born in England in 1745, Asbury, like his parents, cast his lot with John and Charles Wesley, the founders of Methodism. He volunteered for service in the American colonies in 1771. In sharp contrast to virtually all Protestant clergy of the time, who married and settled down in a particular place, Asbury insisted that Methodist ministers must not marry. Instead he expected them to travel from meeting to meeting along a prescribed route as long as the Lord gave them strength to do so. (The Methodists developed their own vocabulary. They called this pattern *itinerating* to *charges* along a *circuit* by a *circuit rider*.)

Asbury himself set the example that would be emulated by thousands of 19th-century circuit riders. The Bishop, as many called him, traveled by horseback, incessantly—in heat and cold, rain and snow—disregarding illness and pain. By the end of his life he had ridden nearly 300,000 miles, crossing the Appalachians more than 60 times and even

HARPER'S WEEKLY.
A
JOURNAL OF CIVILIZATION

Vol. XI.—No. 563.]   NEW YORK, SATURDAY, OCTOBER 12, 1867.   [SINGLE COPY TEN CENTS.
[$4.00 PER YEAR IN ADVANCE.]

Entered according to Act of Congress, in the Year 1867, by Harper & Brothers, in the Clerk's Office of the District Court for the Southern District of New York.

THE CIRCUIT PREACHER.—Drawn by A. R. Waud.—[See next Page.]

This 1867 illustration in *Harper's Weekly* hints at the zeal of Methodist circuit riders. On foot and on horseback, they crisscrossed the nation from Mississippi to New England, from South Carolina to Illinois, establishing outposts of the church.

penetrating into Canada. Some said that Asbury had seen more of the North American continent than any other person of his generation.

Besides carrying the gospel to thousands in backwoods areas of the young republic, Asbury became the prime spokesman for the developing theology of Methodism in the United States. Like most 19th-century revivalists, he insisted that God gave all people the ability to accept God's grace. But he especially emphasized what he saw as the tender, almost mystical, relation between the believer and Christ. Following the model established by John Wesley, Asbury imposed high standards upon converts, prohibiting them from indulging in alcohol and tobacco, and he challenged their growing acceptance of slavery. Most importantly, Asbury, again like Wesley, displayed a clear sense of the importance of good organization. He insisted that power in the church should flow from the top down, not the reverse, as the Baptists and others affected by democratic ideals imagined. Thus Asbury, always the bishop, sent circuit riders where he thought they were needed, when he thought they were needed, with no questions asked. These riders gathered converts into small groups known as classes, defined by age and sex, for worship and mutual support. Classes in turn formed societies, or what other evangelical Protestants called congregations. Even on the frontier, strong organization counted.

The disciplined army of circuit-riding preachers Asbury recruited and dispatched into the seeming wilderness earned a permanent place in the mythology of the American West. Peter Cartwright, for example, stamped his mark on an Illinois circuit with his rough-tongued sermons and willingness physically to pick up and toss out hecklers. When a Presbyterian pastor complained that Cartwright had no right to invade his territory, Cartwright shot back: "I told him the people were a free people and lived in a free country, and must be allowed to do as they pleased." Methodists believed in order, but they also believed that people had a right to choose.

With typical brashness Cartwright ran for Congress in 1846 against an obscure politician named Abraham Lincoln. The preacher lost, but the Methodists won. By the end of the Civil War the once-tiny sect of Methodists had swollen into the largest Protestant denomination in the United States, more than 1 million strong. The Methodists would proudly hold that place until they finally dropped behind the Baptists at the turn of the 20th century.

Asbury's near-contemporary, Charles Grandison Finney, led the Second Great Awakening in the northeast through the 1820s and 1830s. He shouldered the burden of keeping the revival going in the 1820s after Timothy Dwight had passed from the scene. Finney's parents, like thousands of other New England Yankees, had migrated to upstate New York at the beginning of the 19th century. There they reared Finney in a Presbyterian church. In keeping with that denomination's literate tradition, the young Finney studied to practice law. However, he underwent a life-transforming conversion experience in 1821 while reading the Bible in a wooded meadow. Finney later said that he gave up the law because he had received "a retainer from the Lord Jesus Christ to plead his cause." With the help of a local pastor the young preacher taught himself the basics of Puritan theology, though by his own admission he never worried too much about the fine points of it. He soon started preaching in the small towns dotting the Mohawk Valley and then in the larger cities of the region, including Rochester, Rome, and Utica. Eventually Finney settled

A Memorable Call to the Ministry

Evangelist and college president Charles G. Finney preached that a purely intellectual grasp of the doctrines of Christianity was not enough. In his Memoirs (1876), Finney described his own memorable conversion experience and subsequent call to ministry.

Charles Grandison Finney, like many 19th-century evangelical leaders, experienced conversion by himself in the woods. The drawing suggests the light of a supernatural presence.

[The] Holy Spirit descended upon me in a manner that seemed to go through me, body and soul. I could feel the impression, like a wave of electricity, going through and through me. Indeed it seemed to come in waves and waves of liquid love; for I could not express it in any other way. It seemed like the very breath of God. I can recollect distinctly that it seemed to fan me, like immense wings.

No words can express the wonderful love that was shed abroad in my heart. I wept aloud with joy and love; and I do not know but I should say, I literally bellowed out the unutterable gushings of my heart. These waves came over me, and over me, and over me, one after the other, until I recollect I cried out, "I shall die if these waves continue to pass over me." I said, "Lord, I cannot bear any more;" yet I had no fear of death.

in Oberlin, Ohio (near Cleveland), where he taught theology and later served as president of the new Oberlin College.

Finney proved to be notable for several reasons. Like the Wesleys and Asbury, he emphasized the sinner's ability simply to accept God's offer of grace. But more than the others he also stressed the innate ability of men and women to choose good over evil. If they did not, he argued that they should be held responsible. Beyond this insistence, Finney underscored Christians' obligation to consecrate their lives to Christ so fully that they no longer consciously desired to sin. He and others (especially at Oberlin) called this state Christian perfection. They did not mean by it that people would actually be sinless, let alone free of mistakes, but they did mean that perfected Christians would desire to please God over themselves. Finney also earned lasting fame for introducing "New Measures" into revivalism. These New Measures included allowing women to testify (though not to preach) in church, nightly meetings for praise and preaching, and the "anxious bench," a place set aside near the front of the meeting house where sinners could give their lives to Christ.

Like Asbury, Finney stressed the importance of an upright life and of avoiding tobacco, alcohol, dancing, and other recreational activities that might lead to trouble. And Finney, like Asbury, also harbored deep concerns about slavery. Although he did not endorse the views of abolitionists, who seemed extreme at the time, he urged white Christians to find every way possible within the law to restrict the growth of slavery and bring it to an end. Under his administration, Oberlin stood out as the first U.S. college to admit women and blacks. This evangelist did not endorse the formal ordination of women, but he supported women's right to speak in public settings. Each of his three wives (the first two died during his lifetime) distinguished themselves as eloquent proponents of evangelical Christianity, both writing and speaking for the cause. Finney was also an innovator in education. He led the move to drop lectures in favor of class discussion, and urged students to break up the tedium of homework assignments by chopping wood and planting crops.

Unlike the fiery and often unlettered pulpit thumpers of the western camp meetings, as a preacher Finney did not raise his voice or gesture wildly. Tall and physically imposing, he spoke directly, using metaphors drawn from everyday events, especially farm life. He never aimed primarily to arouse his hearers' emotions (although that happened sometimes). His goal rather was to persuade people rationally to confess their sins and embrace Christ's forgiveness. More importantly, he remained convinced that revivals could be cultivated by careful planning. There was nothing miraculous about them, if by miracle one meant "suspending the laws of nature." On the contrary, said Finney in a famous lecture titled "What a Revival of Religion Is," revivals "consist entirely in the *right exercise* of the powers of nature." They resulted from "the right use of the constituted means—as much so as any other effect produced by the application of means."

In later years Finney tempered this view, allowing more leeway for divine influence. But his earlier insistence upon human preparation for revivals stuck in the public mind. By the end of his life Finney had influenced the shape of American religion more than any person since the mid-18th-century leaders John Wesley and Jonathan Edwards.

At this point it may be helpful to pause and think about the major denominational families of the age. Recall that McGready was a Presbyterian, Dwight a Congregationalist, Asbury a Methodist, and Finney a Presbyterian turned Congregationalist. Fortunately, this sequence is not as confusing as it may seem. By the beginning of the 19th century the Presbyterians and Congregationalists had grown virtually identical and, in many places, they simply merged. The Methodists (commonly nicknamed Wesleyans after their founders, the brothers John and Charles Wesley) shared many of the Presbyterian-Congregationalists' basic assumptions. Even so, the Methodists placed more emphasis upon human freedom and on the authority of their bishops. And on the whole, Methodists proved to be more sympathetic to emotional worship and were perhaps less well educated than their Presbyterian-Congregational rivals. At the turn of the century all three groups spearheaded the evangelical revivals. But as the 19th century progressed, a new group of enthusiasts, who had originated in England in the early 17th century, elbowed their way into the picture. They called themselves Baptists.

No one figure led the Baptists' expansion the way that Asbury prompted the Methodists' growth, but the Baptists flourished nonetheless. By the Civil War they ranked as the second-largest Protestant denomination, and they finally overtook the Methodists at the end of the century. The Baptists gained their name because they believed that only adults should be baptized, and baptized by complete immersion, preferably in lakes or rivers. (Children were not to be baptized because they were too young to know what it meant.) In practice, however, the Baptists proved to be more concerned about other matters. They believed that each local church should elect its own pastor and make its own decisions about who should be admitted to membership in their congregations (unlike the Methodists, who received detailed instruction on such matters from their bishops and circuit riders). They also insisted that churches should not

Pavel Svinin, a visiting Russian artist, captured this Protestant baptism ritual near Philadelphia in the early 1800s. On this occasion, solemnity mixed with the chattiness of everyday life.

take tax money from the state. Above all, Baptists yearned to bring sinners to Christ through earnest preaching about the joys of heaven.

The growth of missions represented a natural extension of Baptists' desire to spread the gospel. Yet the missionary impulse, always paramount in the Baptist heart—and wallet—eventually collided with another desire: a determination to protect the institution of slavery. In the 1840s Baptist mission-sponsoring agencies, which were centered in the North, proved to be increasingly reluctant to certify for mission service slave-owning missionaries. As a result, the southern Baptists banded together and in 1845 formed the Southern Baptist Convention. They did so primarily to protect slaveholders' rights in the church. (The Northern Baptists would not organize in a comparable way until 1907.) This rupture prefigured deep trouble to come. If the bonds of Christian fellowship could not hold a denomination together, what could?

The evangelical revival left important legacies in U.S. religious life. One was a new role for women. Although females had always composed a majority of church members, in the years of the awakening they seized the opportunity to speak out as well as up. Dorothy Ripley, an evangelical firebrand from England, earned the distinction of being the first woman to preach in the House of Representatives in 1806 and was probably the first woman to speak in Congress at all. Another evangelical exhorter, Harriet Livermore, the daughter and granddaughter of congressmen, preached in the House on at least four occasions. President John Quincy Adams, who once came to hear her, ended up sitting on the steps to the podium because all the available chairs had been taken.

And then there was Phoebe Palmer, whose life neatly spanned most of the 19th century. By the end of the century it was clear that Palmer stood only slightly behind Asbury and Finney in terms of her long-range influence. Married to a wealthy New York physician, this largely self-taught woman used her considerable financial and intellectual resources to preach the gospel on both sides of the Atlantic. Though Palmer never openly advocated the formal ordination of women, she did strenuously argue, on the basis of Galatians 3:28 ("There is neither . . . male nor female; for you are all one in Christ Jesus") and Joel 2:28 ("Your sons and

FRANK LESLIE'S ILLUSTRATED NEWSPAPER

No. 1,406.—Vol. LV] NEW YORK—FOR THE WEEK ENDING SEPTEMBER 2, 1882. [Price 10 Cents.

In the comparative freedom of the evangelical meeting, women felt comfortable testifying about their own religious experiences. However, very few sought—or received—ordination as clergy.

daughters will prophesy"), that women should enjoy full rights to speak in church and elsewhere of their Christian experience.

The evangelicals left additional legacies. They founded scores of colleges in all parts of the United States. Some of the better known ones include Denison, Kenyon, Knox, Mt. Holyoke, Oberlin, Trinity (now Duke), Tuskegee, and Wheaton (Ill.). By the Civil War, the Baptists and

Methodists alone had sponsored one-third of these schools, and other evangelical groups sponsored and staffed most of the rest.

Many of these schools distinguished themselves for their teaching of what was known as Common Sense morality. This view, drawn from the Scottish universities of the previous century, stressed humans' innate capacity to see the difference between good and bad and then act accordingly. Later philosophers and moralists placed more emphasis upon the ways that culture, always changing, shaped humans' view of the world. In contrast, Common Sense morality focused upon the light of reason, standing above the shifting sands of culture to provide a great beacon to direct the moral life.

Finally, the tradition of evangelical singing and hymns enriched the lives of millions. The Puritans had sung only psalms. Although the Wesleys and other 18th-century hymn-writers penned countless lyrics, these remained stately works emphasizing the community's faith. In contrast, the lively tempos and sentimental lines of typical evangelical songs moved the toes while they stirred the heart. The blind composer Fanny Crosby, who lived for nearly a century, turned out hundreds of songs, many of which are still sung in evangelical churches today. "Rescue the Perishing," "Jesus, Keep Me Near the Cross," and "Blessed Assurance" rank among the well-worn favorites by Crosby.

By 1850 some 70 percent of Protestants belonged to one of the two main evangelical denominations, Baptist or Methodist. Millions more were members of the Presbyterian-Congregationalists, as well as another group called Christians or Disciples of Christ. In a few decades the evangelicals would be sharply challenged by Jews, Roman Catholics, and non-evangelical Protestants like the Lutherans and Episcopalians. But for the better part of the century they dominated American religion and played a large role in public life.

The extraordinary growth in the number of evangelicals in the pre–Civil War years can be explained in a number of ways. One is to see the evangelical message as a response to a deeply felt need for order, following the disorder of the Revolutionary War and the rough-and-tumble whirl of frontier society. Evangelicals' preaching brought regularity to individuals' lives and provided ties of friendship and love among brothers and sisters in the faith. Another explanation for the growth of the movement involves the tie between evangelicalism and rising tides of democratic feeling. In both, individuals held themselves responsible for their behavior and thus their destiny. And finally one can explain the success of evangelicalism in terms of the exceptionally gifted men and women like Asbury, Finney, Palmer, and Crosby, who led the movement. Such individuals asked no one's permission. They simply marched out and took upon themselves the hard work of converting, educating, and morally disciplining the tumultuous world around them. The young republic teemed with hardy religious pioneers, and the evangelicals provided more than their share.

DANIEL'S VISIONS,

"NOTED IN THE SCRIPTURES OF TRUTH," "FOR OUR LEARNING."

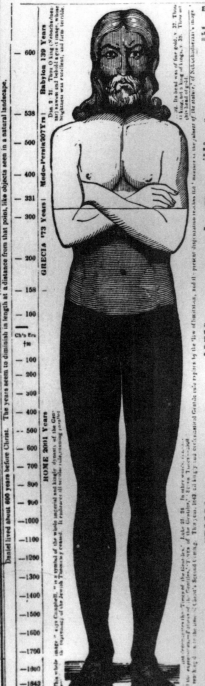

Daniel lived about 600 years before Christ. "The years seem to diminish in length at a distance from that point, like objects seen in a natural landscape.

Babylon 139 Years	Medo-Persia 207 Yrs.	GRECIA "73 Years	ROME 2001 Years

— 600
— 538
— 500
— 400
— 331
— 300
— 200
— 158
— 100

Ch's Era †m

— 100
— 200
— 300
— 400
— 500
— 600
— 700
— 800
— 900
—1000
—1100
—1200
—1300
—1400
—1500
—1600
—1700
—1800
—1843

Dan. 2: 31. Thou O king [Nebuchadnezzar] sawest and behold a great image, whose brightness was excellent, and form was terrible.

37. Thou it king, art a king of kings. v. 38. Thou art this head of gold.

35. Its head was of fine gold, v. 37. Thou O king

"This whole image" "says Campbell, "is a symbol of the whole imperial and kingly dominion of the Gentiles represented of the Jewish Theocracy existed. It embraces all temporal ruling [?] possibly."

BABYLONIAN EMPIRE, B. C. 677. Dan. 7: 4.

In its glory, it was like a lion, soaring with wings as the eagle. But in Belshazzar's time, it had lost its wings and its lion-heart, becoming feeble and faint.

MEDO-PERSIA, B. C. 538. Dan. 7: 5.

The two arms meeting in one breast,—the bear raising up one side, or dominion,—and the ram with two horns, are all appropriate emblems of Medo-Persia. "The Syrian bear, in strength and ferocity scarcely yields to the lion," says Patton. "Ancient historians stigmatize the Medes and Persians as the greatest robbers and spoilers that ever oppressed the nations." The bear represents the nature of the monarchy, but the ram with two horns was its well-known national emblem.

GRECIA, B. C. 331. Dan. 7: 6.

This was founded by Alexander. It was like the leopard, active, crafty and cruel. The lion had 2 wings, but the leopard had 4,—Grecia being more rapid in its conquests than Babylon. But the goat was the known emblem of Greece. It came against the ram with incredible swiftness, making up in speed what it lacked in size. Alexander conquered Persia with a very small army.

ROMAN EMPIRE, B. C. 158. Dan. 7: 7.

"Behold, a fourth beast, dreadful and terrible, and strong exceedingly, which was diverse from all the others, exceeding dreadful, whose teeth were of IRON, and his nails of brass; it devoured, and brake in pieces, and STAMPED the residue with the feet of it. It had ten horns."

THE TEN HORNS.

	A. D.	
1	356	Huns
2	377	Ostrogoths
3	378	Visigoths
4	407	Franks
5	407	Vandals
6	407	Suevi
7	407	Burgundians
8	476	Saxons
9	476	Heruli
0	483	Lombards

"I considered the horns, and behold there came up among them another little horn, before whom there were three of the first horns plucked up by the roots:—that horn had eyes, and a mouth that spake very great things, whose look was more stout [or who was more mighty, as Luther's German Bible reads] than his fellows." Dan. 7: 8.

Papary.

PAPACY, the horn that had eyes (an intelligent seer) arose among the 10, and 3 fell before it. The Heruli in Italy were conquered in 493, the Vandals in 534, & the Ostrogoths were driven from Rome in March, 538.

"This very image" "it is a symbol of the whole imperial and kingly dominion of the Gentiles" [?]

"I beheld, even till the beast was slain, and his body destroyed, and given to the burning flame."

VISION OF THE RAM AND HE GOAT. Dan. 8.

Daniel saw the vision of the ram, he-goat, and exceeding great horn, two years after he saw the representations of the four beasts. According to Lightfoot, Townsend, and other eminent chronologers, it was *after* the fall of Babylon : hence he was " in Shushan," the capital of Persia. Babylon being then a subject of history, had no place in this prophecy.

"Behold, a ram which had two horns, and the two horns were high, but the higher came up last." The ram which came from the east, with its two horns, was Media and Persia ; and the rough goat which darted upon him from the west, was Grecia—so said the angel. The Grecian empire was at first united, as is represented by the single horn of the goat. It was afterwards divided into four parts, represented by the four horns, of which the angel said—"Four KINGDOMS shall stand up out of the nation." Here we are taught, in the plainest manner, that a horn in this vision means a kingdom.

MEDO-PERSIA.

GRECIA.

Enlarged View of the Four Horns.

After the death of Alexander, Grecia was divided into four parts, toward the four Winds of heaven. v. 8. And out of one of them, came forth a little horn, which waxed EXCEEDING great. (v. 9.) even to the host of heaven. v 10

In chapter 2, Rome is represented by the feet and legs of the image. In chapter 7, it is represented by the fourth Beast having ten horns. But in the 8th chapter it is symbolized by an EXCEEDING great horn.

That this exceeding great horn represents Rome, is evident from the following and many other reasons.

1. It rises "In the latter part of their kingdom,"—that is, of the four kingdoms. So did Rome, as far as its place in the prophecy is concerned. Its connection with the Jews commenced 158 years before Christ.

2. It was "of fierce countenance." So was Rome—See Deut. 28: 49, 50.

3. It was "little" at first. So was Rome.

4. It waxed "exceeding great," towards the east and towards the south." So did Rome.

"From this horn increasing towards the *south* and *east*, particularly Sir Isaac Newton sagaciously infers, that it arose in the northwest corner of the Goat's dominion, i. e. in Italy—which points directly to the Romans."

5. It cast down some of the host and of the stars to the ground. So did Rome :—persecuting Christians, Apostles and ministers of Jesus, as no other power ever did.

6. "He magnified himself even to the Prince of the host." So did Rome, when the Pope became the "head of all the churches." But the margin reads more properly, "He magnified himself AGAINST the PRINCE of the host," and in the interpretation the angel says, "He shall stand up against the PRINCE of princes." Thus did Rome, when both Herod and Pontius Pilate conspired against the holy Jesus.

7. "He shall destroy wonderfully, and shall destroy the mighty and holy people." Thus did Rome.

Chapter 3

Visionaries

Stand up, stand up for Jesus, ye soldiers of the cross;
Lift high his royal banner, it must not suffer loss.
From victory unto victory his army shall he lead,
till every foe is vanquished, and Christ is Lord indeed.
  —*George Duffield Jr., "Stand Up, Stand Up for Jesus" (1858)*

"We are all a little wild here with numberless projects of social reform" was the way essayist Ralph Waldo Emerson described American religion to an English friend in 1840. Every reading person, Emerson continued, seemed to hold "a draft of a new community in his waistcoat pocket." In one sense Emerson was simply stating the obvious. For the better part of 2000 years Christians had tried to help the needy, and the same held true for Christians in colonial America. In the 16th century Roman Catholic friars had come to New Spain—now the Gulf Coast states and New Mexico—partly to spread the benefits of Christian civilization. The Puritans journeyed to New England a century later, for some of the same reasons. They hoped to establish a justly ordered society in which the widow, the orphan, and the pauper would receive proper care. The Quakers, who started migrating to the middle colonies of Delaware, New Jersey, and Pennsylvania in the late 17th century, went further. They called for pacifism, humane treatment of the Indians, the temperate use of alcohol, and sanctions against slaveholders and slave traders. Nonetheless, these Christians

William Miller's followers used elaborate drawings, like this 1843 chart, to help Christians understand the complex predictions about the end of the world that the followers saw in the biblical books of Daniel, Ezekiel, and Revelation.

thought in terms of relief, not reform. They assumed that poverty and pain were here to stay. For the most part, the best one could do was to ease the suffering. The idea of making fundamental changes in society lay beyond their ken.

In the early 19th century a new approach to poverty and human suffering began to emerge. By that point in the industrial revolution it was clear that capitalism had created great inequalities. But it also opened up people's mental horizons, persuading many that the world really could be fundamentally improved. Rationalists like Thomas Jefferson had taught that society, no less than nature, was subject to its own laws. By mastering those laws individuals could make life more just, more humane, indeed, more enjoyable. Above all, thoughtful men and women began to believe that human beings were not always and everywhere shackled by the chains of selfishness. Increasingly, a grandly biblical vision of self-sacrifice in the interests of others seemed truly possible. All these trends flowed together at the beginning of the 19th century. Little wonder that thousands of people, religious and otherwise, would begin to come up with fresh ideas for making this new American world a better place to live.

The decades between the turn of the 19th century and the opening of the Civil War witnessed an explosion of reform efforts. The largest and most systematic projects—centering in the 1820s and 1830s—stemmed from broadly evangelical groups, first the Congregationalists and Presbyterians, then the Baptists and Methodists. They took their cues from similar endeavors in Britain. The British groups sought to combat evils like slavery, prostitution, alcoholism, and poverty. They won the support of the most powerful and prestigious citizens, including Parliament member William Wilberforce, who belonged to 69 reform societies and helped to end the British slave trade in 1807.

The U.S. crusade first concentrated on spreading Christianity and civilization to the West, to the backwoods regions of the South, and to non-Christian lands overseas. In 1810, for example, Samuel J. Mills Jr., a student at Williams College and later at Andover Seminary (both in Massachusetts), helped organize a voluntary agency called the American Board of Commissioners for Foreign Missions. Many, including Mills

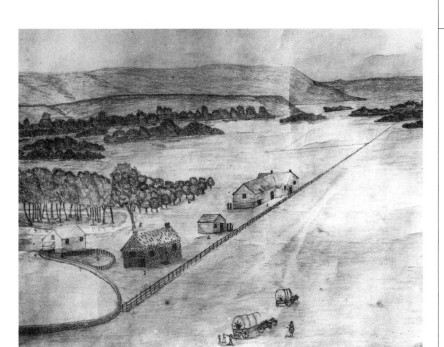

In the 1840s Presbyterian missionaries Marcus and Narcissa Whitman pushed deep into unknown territory to carry the Christian gospel to Native Americans. The famed Oregon Trail ran alongside the fence around the Whitmans' mission, pictured here before the massacre.

himself, whose health prevented him from going overseas, concentrated on evangelizing the American West. For example, in the 1830s Methodist missionary Jason Lee carried the gospel message to the Flathead Indians of the Pacific Northwest. The Presbyterian missionaries Marcus and Narcissa Whitman soon followed. Their deaths at the hands of Indians in 1847 increased public concern about the West. Hundreds of missionaries and then pastors, including many women, followed.

Evangelicals regarded the South too as a mission field, one desperately needing reform. And with good reason. Until the middle of the century probably the majority of southerners remained unchurched. The Episcopal church, dominant during the colonial era, had come to be identified with the privileges of the planter aristocracy. Moreover, a "culture of honor," which placed a premium upon drinking, gambling, dueling, aggressive sports, and male sexual conquests, pervaded the Old South. Evangelical religion, espoused especially by lower- and lower-middle-class whites and slaves, challenged the culture of honor. Evangelicals esteemed humility, frugality, sexual chastity, humane treatment of slaves, mutual accountability, and "sweet fellowship" in Christ.

Father Pierre Jean De Smet's Work with the Sioux

Christian missionaries, both at home and abroad, often experienced hardship in the pursuit of their ideals. In this 1864 letter to the archbishop of Cincinnati, U.S. Army Major General David S. Stanley described the work of Father Pierre Jean De Smet, a Jesuit missionary to the Sioux.

The Reverend Father is known among the Indians by the name of "Blackrobe" and "Big Medicine Man." . . . He is the only man for whom I have ever seen Indians evince a real affection. They say, in their simple and open language, that he is the only white man who has not a forked tongue; that is, who never lies to them. . . .

[We] can never forget nor shall we ever cease to admire, the disinterested devotion of the Reverend Father De Smet, who, at the age of sixty-eight years, did not hesitate, in the midst of the heat of summer, to undertake a long and perilous journey, across the burning plains, destitute of trees and even of grass; having none but corrupted and unwholesome water, constantly exposed to scalping by Indians, and this without seeking either honors or remuneration of any sort; but solely to arrest the shedding of blood and save, if it might be, some lives, and preserve some habitations to these savage children of the desert, to whose spiritual and temporal welfare he has consecrated a long life of labor and solicitude.

Besides missions, evangelical reformers spearheaded the growth of literacy in general and Bible knowledge in particular. For example, they formed the American Sunday School Union in 1824. It supplied libraries with spelling books, alphabetical cards, and tens of thousands of books. Voluntary societies launched more than 700,000 new Sunday schools in the 19th century, many of which provided general and religious instruction for frontier children. After the Civil War, Sunday schools all over the land adopted a standardized Uniform Lesson Plan, so that children would study the same Bible passages nationwide each week. Other agencies distributed Bibles and tracts. By 1815, 100 such agencies existed, then merged the following year into the American Bible Society.

Tract societies followed the same pattern, first organizing locally, then combining into the nationwide American Tract Society in 1825. The sheer number of pages that its partisans distributed without charge was startling by any standards. Between 1829 and 1831, for example, the American Tract Society turned out 65 million pages of tracts, five pages for every person in America. Successive editions of *Eclectic Readers*, edited by the Presbyterian minister William Holmes McGuffey, dominated public school classrooms in the Midwest and elsewhere for the better part of a century, eventually selling 122 million copies. Although these readers purported to be nondenominational, they presented stories saturated with evangelical values of sobriety, hard work, punctuality, and respectfulness toward elders and persons in authority. Evangelical values also passed into the general culture through popular magazines such as *Godey's Lady's Book*.

The abuse of alcohol captured reformers' attention too. From the beginning Quakers had targeted alcohol's evils, but to little avail. Drinking

With the availability of cheap printing, reformers believed that the tract (a kind of pamphlet) offered the perfect medium for changing popular habits. This American Tract Society flyer indicates the class differences between the well scrubbed tract giver and his wife, and the aproned tract receiver burdened by children.

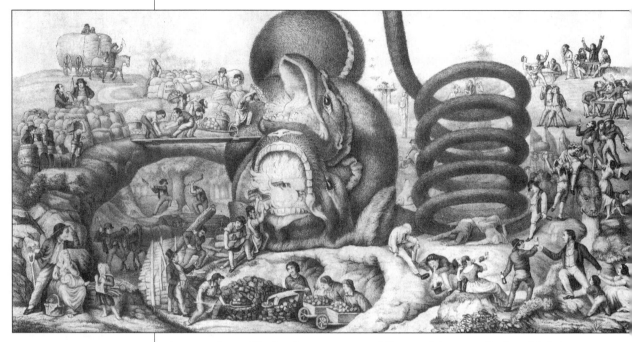

This temperance chart, probably from the middle 19th century, contrasts the benefits of remaining sober against the perils of drunkenness. The dragon of alcohol destroys those who are not careful.

increased steadily in the young republic, reaching an all-time high by 1830. Critics of drink organized the Society for the Promotion of Temperance in 1826. As growing industrialization and urbanization raised the risks of intoxication, the older call for moderation gave way to a demand for total abstinence. In the 1830s certain localities started banning liquor. (Some of these so-called dry towns maintain similar bans even today.) In 1836 reformers formed the American Temperance Union. Ten years later Maine became the first state to pass statewide prohibition. The temperance crusade sputtered in the Civil War decade, but arose again with force in the last third of the century, leading to nationwide Prohibition in the 1920s. The later crusade captured the enthusiasm of reformers across the political and religious spectrum, enlisting conservative and liberal alike.

The growing determination to effect more equal treatment for women proved to be a great deal more controversial than the temperance issue. Evangelical and non-evangelical women alike first organized themselves into female antislavery societies in the early 1830s. Soon some women, including the Quaker sisters Sarah and Angelina Grimke, started speaking publicly against slavery. This practice provoked a bitter confrontation within the antislavery ranks. Should women be allowed to mount a platform and address men publicly, as equals? The majority of abolitionists said no, opposing the notion as untimely at best and fundamentally wrong at worst. But a few said yes. For example, in 1848 Elizabeth Cady Stanton and Lucretia Mott organized a Women's Rights Convention. Although Stanton had been reared in a strict Presbyterian home, by then she had grown deeply skeptical of traditional Christianity. And Mott regarded herself a liberal Quaker. These and other advocates chose to meet in an evangelical Wesleyan Methodist Church in Seneca Falls, New York, where they would continue to meet throughout the 1850s.

Activist Christians formed many more voluntary groups for the reform of society. Some called for pacifism, others for the humane treatment of prisoners, some to establish asylums for the blind, still others for the abolition of cruel practices like dueling, which had taken the life of Alexander Hamilton and nearly that of Abraham Lincoln too. Other well-known societies of the time included the American Colonization Society (for resettling freed slaves in Liberia), the American Home Missionary Society, the American Education Society, and the American Antislavery Society. Friends dubbed the growing network of reform societies the Benevolent Empire. They had good reason, for at one point the Benevolent Empire boasted a budget larger than that of the federal government!

A small number of farsighted men and women, often wealthy and well educated, basically ran the operations of the Benevolent Empire out of offices in New York City. Two of the most prominent included the Tappan brothers, Arthur and Lewis. As prosperous New York silk merchants the Tappans financed a variety of antebellum reform projects. For instance, when the new Oberlin College came under heavy attack for admitting students with antislavery views, they kept the school going. They also supported sabbath observance, temperance, and the abolition of slavery. Lewis Tappan in particular represented the changing outlook of evangelical Protestants. As a young man, Puritanlike notions of divine sovereignty and human sinfulness had occupied his attention. As a mature man, however, Lewis showed increasing interest in the happiness of humankind and moral order in society.

Some of the major reform efforts of the antebellum years stemmed from liberal rather than evangelical Christian traditions. The Unitarians in particular offered a non-evangelical route to social reform. Formally organized in 1825, the Unitarians took their name from their insistence on God's essential unity (versus God as trinity). In practice, however, they proved to be primarily interested in individuals' ability to change themselves and the world for the better. For example, Horace Mann, a Unitarian educator in Massachusetts, helped to establish free schools for children in his home state and throughout the United States. He vigorously combated slavery, liquor, tobacco, lotteries, profanity, and dancing, all on the ground that these activities did people more harm than good. Like many other liberal reformers, Mann retained the moral energy of the old New England Puritan tradition even as he let the formal theology slip away.

Dorothea Dix, another Unitarian reformer, proved to be even more influential than Mann. Reared in the home of a strict Methodist minister just after the turn of the century, Dix gravitated toward the religious liberalism of a Harvard-educated uncle. Though Dix never doubted the truth of the Bible or the divinity of Jesus, she came to believe that Christianity's essence lay in Jesus' command to feed the poor and comfort the sick. For several decades Dix, who never married, wandered from one genteel vocation to another. She taught school and wrote children's books and uplifting adult fiction. But in 1843 things changed dramatically for her. A stint teaching Sunday school in a Boston-area jail left her appalled at the shocking conditions there, especially the mixing of ordinary criminals with the insane. Dix had found her life's work. In the next 30 years she would visit all of the jails, almshouses (poorhouses), and private homes for the mad in New England, documenting their squalid surroundings and forcing legislatures to make major reforms. In all, Dix spearheaded the founding or expansion of 32 mental hospitals in 15 states, Canada, Britain, continental Europe, and Japan. Additionally, after the outbreak of the Civil War, Dix became Superintendent of Women Nurses, the highest office held by a woman in the Union Army.

Dix's career proved to be instructive in another respect. Though she awakened the nation to the plight of the mad, she held conservative views about the place of women in society and remained aloof from the antislavery crusade. By any reasonable measure of such things, this New England reformer was a great woman. But her vision, like that of all reformers, was structured by the limitations of her time and place.

The reform impulses growing out of the dominant forms of Christianity, both evangelical and liberal, shared the landscape with alternate visions that emerged outside the boundaries of mainline Christianity. Some, such as the Millerites, straddled the border, drawing upon historically Christian concerns but taking them further than most Americans wanted to go. Others, such as the Shakers and the Oneida Perfectionists, moved far beyond Christianity's boundaries. Most such groups hoped to reconstruct society in more humane ways. Though scores of such groups emerged in the antebellum years, the three just named deserve a closer look, for they represented distinctive tiles in the larger mosaic.

The 19th century knew many self-educated Bible scholars and homegrown philosophers. One of the most imaginative and influential such figures was the New York farmer William Miller. In the 1830s Miller dropped his plow to take up exhorting in Baptist churches. But he was no ordinary preacher. Intensive study of Scripture, especially the numerical codes in the book of Daniel, led him to conclude that the Lord would probably return on March 21, 1843. This prophet's interest in numbers

This 1861 letter from the Secretary of War outlines the duties of Dorothea Dix as Superintendent of Women Nurses for the Union Army. Her responsibilities included organizing military hospitals, providing nurses where they were needed, and dispensing supplies and donations to the soldiers.

may have reflected Americans' growing interest in technology, which depended upon making precise mathematical calculations. It also showed a growing conviction that the Bible held all the answers, which humans could decipher if they only studied it hard enough. Miller's message spread rapidly through his periodicals—significantly titled *The Midnight Cry* and *Signs of the Times*—as well as 5 million copies of tracts and booklets. His views reached a broad audience in Horace Greeley's *New York Herald,* complete with illustrations. Comets and meteor showers at the time added to the excitement. Some said that Miller attracted 30,000 to 100,000 followers. When the longed-for return of the Lord did not materialize in 1843, Miller changed the date to October 22, 1844. When that uneventful night also passed, most of his followers drifted away, brokenhearted. Miller himself and a handful of faithful disciples remained certain that they had only made a calculation error and that Christ would return shortly. Others reorganized themselves as an enduring sect called the Seventh-day Adventists.

How did the Millerites advance social reform? In one sense not at all, for they expected the Lord suddenly to bring history to a crashing end. But in another sense they did, for they opposed slavery and all other activities they saw as harmful that prevented men and women from being ready for Christ's return. After his death, Miller's followers embraced a broad range of health reforms as well, involving strict notions of proper diet, rest, exercise, dress, and sexual discipline. Beyond that, the Millerites displayed a fierce optimism about the course of history. Most evangelicals felt responsibility for creating the Kingdom of God on the North American continent in their lifetimes. Miller's vision was even grander. For him the Lord was coming back any day. He would enlist believers in the exhilarating work of creating the New Heavens and the New Earth, making all things right.

A second visionary movement with an end-times message took the ponderous name of the United Society of Believers in Christ's Second Appearance. Mother Ann Lee, as her followers called her, started the sect among plain folk in England in the mid-1700s. A cook and washerwoman, Lee remained illiterate all her life. After her four children died in infancy, she came to the conclusion that all sexual activity, whether in or out of marriage, equaled sin. She argued that the path to salvation therefore started with celibacy (abstaining from sex). Eventually, Lee joined a band of Quakers whose chosen mode of worship involved whirling and trembling, or "shaking off their sins." And so it was that they came to be known as Shakers. Lee's band migrated to upstate New York in 1774. Within a decade Lee died from injuries inflicted by hostile neighbors, but her followers proclaimed the message of salvation through celibacy northward into New England and southward into Ohio and Kentucky.

The movement grew luxuriantly in the experimental atmosphere of pre–Civil War America. At their peak the Shaker communities or colonies numbered 5,000 adherents altogether. The Shakers regarded Lee herself as the incarnation of the Second Coming of Christ, the Holy Mother Wisdom. Shaker men and women maintained strict equality, with two male and two female leaders in charge of each group. The adherents worked side by side, sharing all things except minor personal items in common. They reproduced themselves by adopting orphans, many of whom stayed in the community upon reaching adulthood. They opposed slavery, dressed plainly, and refused to fight. Shaker worship centered in ritualized or highly structured dancing that could go on for hours as a form of worship before the Lord.

Perhaps the most noted feature of the Shaker community was a scrupulous attention to simplicity, cleanliness, and usefulness. These traits found expression in the Shakers' furniture and in the simple lines of their buildings. In the mid-19th century the Shakers embodied a powerful vision of what a carefully ordered society, free of sexual desire, greed, or waste, might look like. At the end of the 20th century only a handful of Shakers remained, all at Sabbathday Lake, Maine.

The Oneida Perfectionists, located in the small upstate New York village of Oneida, embodied a third visionary movement. The Perfectionists grew out of the labors of John Humphrey Noyes. Born in Vermont in 1811, Noyes attended Dartmouth College, where he underwent a

This 1848 woodcut of a Shaker dance suggests that hours of rhythmic dancing may have encouraged trances and inspired prophecies.

memorable evangelical conversion experience. He then went on to Andover Seminary and Yale Divinity School. At Yale, however, he found himself in considerable trouble for claiming—contrary to 2,000 years of Christian teaching—that he had achieved a state of Christian perfection, untainted by any residue of sin. This state was possible, he argued, because Christ had returned in A.D. 70 and given the church the power of his spirit. In 1841 Noyes established a community of followers in Putney, Vermont. They too pursued earthly perfection, expressed through economic sharing, divine healing, the mutual confession of sins (except by Noyes himself), and "complex marriage." The last involved the systematic rotation of husbands and wives among members of the community, based on the assumption that perfected people should share all things, including spouses.

Opposition from neighbors forced the community to relocate to Oneida, New York, in 1848. Undeterred, Noyes eventually instituted a still more radical plan of selecting a small number of men and women deemed worthy for breeding. In New York the business-savvy Perfectionists grew prosperous through the manufacture of steel animal traps, travel bags, and silver-plated flatware. Although by the late 1870s the settlement had dwindled to only 250 residents, neighbors had seen enough. Noyes escaped to Canada in 1879 and the community formally dissolved two years later. But the Perfectionists' notoriety long outlived them. Oneida silverware, now produced by a secular corporation, persists as a tangible reminder of one of the longest lived and most radical of all U.S. reform experiments.

All three of these groups emerged about the same time and in roughly the same area: western New York State, sometimes called the Burned Over District because of the succession of revival preachers and radical groups that blazed across the region. All of them tinkered with conventional notions of time by reconceiving the date of Christ's return. And all challenged conventional ideas of ownership: the Millerites regarding slaves, the Perfectionists and Shakers concerning private property. The latter two groups also reworked time-honored notions of family relations, but in opposite ways. All three represented a new vision, fired by the religious imagination, of better social arrangements.

Many, though not all, of these reform impulses flowed together in the life of one singularly influential woman. Her real name was Isabella Baumfree, but by the time of her death most Americans knew her as Sojourner Truth. By whatever name, she showed how fairly conventional ideas about reform could merge with some very radical ones.

Born a slave in upstate New York about 1797, Baumfree was torn from her birth family and sold twice while yet a child. She reached adulthood in a Dutch-speaking family, and thus spoke English with a Dutch accent the rest of her life. During that time she embraced a strict Methodist faith. Freed by her owner at the age of 30, Baumfree moved to New York City, where she allied herself with a religious prophet named Elijah Pierson. He had established a commune calling for equality between men and women, between blacks and whites, and between wealthy and poor. This commune, known as the Kingdom of Matthias, did not last long, partly because Pierson was unable to live up to his own ideals. In the meantime, Baumfree received a vision from the Lord directing her to travel the land preaching a message of personal salvation, abolition of slavery, equal rights for women, and justice for the poor.

John Humphrey Noyes, founder of the Oneida Perfectionists, evoked loyalty from followers and fear and loathing from neighbors. His complex theological ideas included the sharing of property and of marriage partners.

"I sell the shadow to support the substance." With these words Sojourner Truth, an ex-slave, marketed photos of herself to support her efforts to promote racial and women's equality.

Because she believed herself a traveling messenger for the Lord, the name Sojourner Truth came to Baumfree naturally. Tall, bony, and articulate, she cut a dramatic figure on the lecture circuit. Hecklers, amused to see a black woman speaking publicly, got more than they bargained for with her quick-witted retorts. Truth lobbied President Abraham Lincoln on behalf of the slaves. After the war, she worked tirelessly for government policies to protect, educate, and resettle newly freed black men and women. She lobbied for hospitals and orphanages for former bondsmen. At the same time, she pressed former slaves to take responsibility for their own welfare. It was almost inevitable that Truth would finally end up in Battle Creek, Michigan, a center of late-19th-century efforts to improve health by reforming diet, dress, and hygiene.

Why did the reform impulse emerge most often among groups that traced their roots back to the Protestant Reformation in England—the Congregationalists, Presbyterians, Quakers, Baptists, Methodists, and Unitarians? (The same pattern proved true of radical groups too. The Millerites stemmed from the Baptists, the Shakers from the Quakers, and the Oneida Perfectionists from the Methodists.) Several answers are possible. Traditionally, English Protestant groups emphasized the parts of the Bible that spoke of responsibility to the whole of society. Also, members of those groups tended to be well educated and economically secure, which gave them both the vision and the means to help others. In contrast, a large minority of Christians, including Roman Catholics, Lutherans, and Mennonites, as well as Jews, rarely attempted to reform society as a whole. This was not because they were selfish but because they were confronted by the more pressing problems of taking care of their own families in a forbidding land.

This point raises a final question. How did the subjects—or rather the objects, we might better say—of the reformers' efforts feel about all the attention on their behalf? Some clearly appreciated the extended hand, but others resented the real or perceived interference in their lives. They saw the visionaries not as heroes but as do-gooders and busybodies. Echoes of that conversation persist today in debates about abortion and drug use. One side seeks to change the world for the better while the other side asks, who is to define what is "better"?

Shortly we shall look at the greatest reform crusade of all, the war to end slavery. That effort would take more than words, money, and sweat, however. It would cost lives—more than a half million of them. But before turning to the antislavery crusade, we need to look at two other major groups that also emerged in the mid-19th century. Each manifested its own distinctive set of concerns; each made its own distinctive mark upon the American religious landscape.

Chapter 4

Restorers

The Spirit of God like a fire is burning;
The latter-day glory begins to come forth;
The visions and blessings of old are returning;
The angels are coming to visit the earth.
We'll sing and we'll shout with the armies of heaven,
"Hosannah, hosannah to God and the Lamb!"
　　—W. W. Phelps, *"The Spirit of God Like a Fire Is Burning"* (c. 1830)

In the second quarter of the 19th century thousands of Americans sought progress not by looking forward to the end of history but by looking backward to its beginning. Some wanted to restore the perfect order they saw in the New Testament. They called themselves simply Christians, or occasionally Disciples of Christ. Others, more radical, wanted to restore the perfect order they read about in both the Old and the New Testaments. The Church of Jesus Christ of Latter-day Saints, better known as the Mormons, formed the largest and most influential example.

The Christian movement began in two places. The first stirrings occurred in northern Kentucky, the second in western Pennsylvania. In Kentucky, just after the turn of the century, Presbyterian preacher Barton W. Stone cast his lot with the revivals taking place near Cane Ridge, discussed in Chapter 2. Although Cane Ridge had gained a reputation for unrestrained expression of religious emotion, Stone supported its revivals for a different reason. He believed they freed people from oppressive control by denominational officials, giving them the right to worship when,

In 1892 the temple of the Latter-day Saints in Salt Lake City, Utah, undoubtedly ranked as the most impressive building between the Rocky Mountains and California. Today there are Mormon temples in countries around the world.

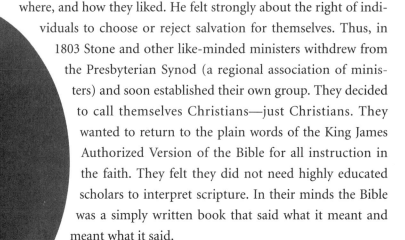

Clear-eyed and strong-willed, Alexander Campbell stamped his personality on the Christian Churches/Disciples of Christ. He taught that believers should ignore all the quarreling between different religious sects and simply read the New Testament for its clear teachings.

where, and how they liked. He felt strongly about the right of individuals to choose or reject salvation for themselves. Thus, in 1803 Stone and other like-minded ministers withdrew from the Presbyterian Synod (a regional association of ministers) and soon established their own group. They decided to call themselves Christians—just Christians. They wanted to return to the plain words of the King James Authorized Version of the Bible for all instruction in the faith. They felt they did not need highly educated scholars to interpret scripture. In their minds the Bible was a simply written book that said what it meant and meant what it said.

About this same time, a Scottish immigrant in western Pennsylvania named Alexander Campbell also abandoned the Presbyterian church. Campbell was a brilliant though argumentative young man. Like Stone, Campbell felt that all people should be able to choose their own church, select their own pastor, and read the Bible in their own way. Campbell believed that the New Testament, and the New Testament alone, should serve as a blueprint for all things that Christians believed and did in the present—not the traditions of the church and not the speculations of school-taught theologians. His motto was: "Where the Scriptures speak, we speak; where the Scriptures are silent, we are silent." Read the Bible, he said, as if mortal eyes had never seen it before. In addition, Campbell felt that by using the New Testament alone as a guide, believers could avoid all the squabbling about which church was right. If they would only look to the Scripture, and not at human interpretations of it, there would be no more divisions or fighting. Campbell's followers sometimes called themselves Christians and at others Disciples of Christ, in order to emphasize the simplicity and unifying power of their message.

Various ideas circulating within the antebellum culture of the United States influenced both of these groups, the Stoneites in Kentucky and the Campbellites in Pennsylvania. Specifically, their emphasis upon the right of ordinary persons to make decisions for themselves in matters of religious belief and church government found an echo in the ideals of President Andrew Jackson, which emphasized the right of ordinary people to make crucial decisions for themselves in matters of political belief and civil government. Both the Stoneites and Campbellites evinced a strong dislike of intellectual elites. They particularly scorned the pretense of well-born and well-educated people (especially those from the East) to make decisions on behalf of plain folk (especially those from the West).

In one important respect, however, the growing Christian movement departed from broad trends in the culture and from other evangelical denominations. The Christians avoided the open display of religious emotion. Their converts did not need to go through an intense conversion experience, marked by weeping or groaning or uncontrolled behavior. All they needed was to read the Bible, believe what it said, repent of their sins, and be baptized by immersion as a mark of obedience.

By the early 1830s the Stoneites and the Campbellites realized that they shared many ideas and practices. Consequently, they informally united in Lexington, Kentucky, in 1832, bringing together some 13,000 supporters. They went by various names: Christians, Disciples of Christ, or Restorationists. (The last term emerged because they aimed to restore the patterns of the New Testament church.) These three labels were interchangeable.

Toward the end of the century things grew even more confusing when the Christians split into a definably northern branch, by then usually called the Christian Church/Disciples of Christ, and an identifiably southern branch, by that time usually known as the Churches of Christ. Together they claimed about 650,000 adherents. Although the Christian movement never grew as large as the closely related evangelical one, it nevertheless represented one of the more impressive traditions to be born on American soil in the 19th century. Its hallmarks included restorationist fervor, radical democracy, and an enduring confidence in the power of individuals to think clearly and choose truth for themselves.

The Mormons, a second major group of "restorers" who arose in the 19th century, grew much larger and proved to be considerably more radical than the Christians. The story of the Mormons was, and remains, tied to the life of their founder, Joseph Smith, Jr. Born in 1805, young Joseph matured in difficult circumstances. His father's farming efforts in Vermont met with little success because of bad weather and rocky soil. Thus, in 1816 the Smith family, along with thousands of other struggling New Englanders, pulled up stakes and migrated westward. They settled in the small town of Palmyra, New York, in the north-central region of the state. Economic ups and downs, coupled with intense religious unrest, marked the area. In New York both father and son worked at a variety of jobs, possibly including efforts to find buried treasure with a magical seer stone. Over time the Smiths' fortunes improved, but they never knew real economic security.

Joseph's adolescent life proved to be troubled in other respects too. Neither of his parents was securely tied to any of the main Christian groups of the region. The senior Smith considered himself something of a freethinker, but he was never too sure about his unbelief. Joseph's mother, Lucy Mack Smith, regarded herself a Presbyterian, but she also seemed unclear of her commitments. For Lucy, too many different groups claimed to know the truth. Joseph inherited his parents' uncertainty about the current religious choices. But more than either of them he determined to settle the truth for himself.

Many years later Joseph told his own story. He said that one day in 1820, just before his 15th birthday, he was praying by himself in the woods. He asked God to show him which church was right. One day God the Father and Jesus Christ the Son appeared to him in a vision. They told him that none was right. The early Christians had lost the truth through sinful behavior and, once it was lost, there was no hope for finding it again until God restored it. Over the next seven years (between the ages of 14 and 21) young Smith experienced additional visions. The most important came in the fall of 1823 when the angel Moroni (an angel unique to Smith, and not existing in other Christian traditions) visited him. Moroni told Joseph about a set of golden tablets hidden beneath a stone on a nearby hillside, which held the wisdom he was seeking. In 1827 Moroni instructed Joseph to retrieve the tablets and translate what was written on

God's Messenger Moroni Visits Joseph Smith

In September of 1823, at the age of 17, Joseph Smith experienced one of several visions that led him to abandon all the prevailing forms of Christianity in favor of a new one. In an autobiographical reminiscence written 15 years later, History of Joseph Smith, by Himself, *the Prophet described the events that led to the discovery, translation, and publication of the* Book of Mormon.

I discovered a light appearing in the room, which continued to increase until the room was lighter than at noonday, when immediately a personage appeared at my bedside, standing in the air, for his feet did not touch the floor. He had on a loose robe of most exquisite whiteness. It was a whiteness beyond anything earthly I had ever seen; nor do I believe that any earthly thing could be made to appear so exceedingly white and brilliant. . . .

When I first looked upon him I was afraid, but the fear soon left me. He called me by name and said unto me that he was a messenger sent from the presence of God to me, and that his name was Moroni. That God had a work for me to do, and that my name should be had for good and evil among all nations, kindreds, and tongues. . . . He said that there was a book deposited, written upon gold plates, giving an account of the former inhabitants of this continent, and the source from whence they sprang. He also said that the fullness of the everlasting Gospel was contained in it, as delivered by the Savior to the ancient inhabitants. Also, that there were two stones in silver bows . . . deposited with the plates, and the possession and use of these stones was what constituted seers in ancient or former times, and that God had prepared them for the purpose of translating the book.

them (in a lost language called Reformed Egyptian). Joseph recalled that he sat on one side of a curtain and deciphered each word, while Emma, his young bride, and two or three others sat on the other side writing down his remarks. He was only allowed to show the tablets to 11 other people named by Moroni.

By March 1830 the translation was complete. Smith found a printer and published the work as the *Book of Mormon.* Although Mark Twain would call it "chloroform in print," the volume bore many resemblances in theme and style to the beloved King James Authorized Version of the Bible. About 500 pages long, it featured an epic story much like the sagas recounted in the Old Testament.

According to the *Book of Mormon,* ancient peoples of Hebrew extraction came to the New World on barges about 600 B.C. settling in Central America. The leader was Lehi, a patriarch very much like the biblical Abraham. Lehi's sons divided into two clans, the Nephites and the Lamanites. Though both groups had their failings, on the whole the Nephites proved to be righteous, while the Lamanites did not. The tribes struggled against each other for centuries. Jesus Christ visited these New World Hebrews after his resurrection, offering them the message of salvation, but the conflicts persisted into the fourth century. Finally, in a terrible battle very much like the battle of Armageddon described in the New Testament Book of Revelation the Lamanites slew all but two of the Nephites: the great warrior Mormon, and his son Moroni. Mormon then wrote the story of these New World argonauts on the golden plates. In A.D. 384 Moroni hid them on the hillside near Palmyra, New York, where Smith ultimately found them. In the meantime the victorious Lamanites became increasingly dark skinned and ignorant. Their descendants formed the Indians whom the Europeans encountered a thousand years later.

It is hard to know how to account for the *Book of Mormon*'s origin or its success. Smith had received little formal education. How then could he write so much in such a short time? For those who became Mormons, the book contained a direct revelation from God proclaimed by God's specially selected prophet. For those who did not, the book represented great religious imagination at best, or outright fraud at worst. Whatever one believed about the authorship of the book, the volume clearly offered answers to questions people of the 1830s were asking about their new continent. It explained signs of advanced civilization in Central America, such as pyramids and elaborate stone calendars. It accounted for the origins of the Indians. It gave citizens of the United States, anxious about their lack of deep historical roots, a secure place in the grand scheme of things. Above all, it helped believers see America itself as a uniquely chosen place, for God had selected Americans to serve as the carriers of a restored gospel.

Scores of hardworking plain folk soon flocked to Smith. He organized them into the Church of Jesus Christ (later adding "of Latter-day Saints" to the title). But opposition arose, partly because other Christians, whom the Mormons called Gentiles, strongly resisted the idea that any collection of writings outside the Bible should be considered equal to the Bible. They also doubted that God would single out an ordinary person like the roughly hewn Smith to receive new revelation. To escape harassment, Joseph and Emma Smith and a small band of followers moved to Kirtland, Ohio, near Cleveland, in 1831. There they built a temple, and Smith began to receive additional direct revelations about doctrinal matters. Some of these had to do with the nature of God (who was material), humans (who were gods in the making), and marriage (to be patterned after the Old Testament model of multiple wives). For a short time the Mormons also tried to abolish private ownership of property, calling for the sharing of material and economic resources.

Opposition continued to dog the Mormons even in Ohio. Once a group of ruffians dragged Smith from his home and tarred and feathered him. So in 1838 many members of the sect moved on to Missouri, where they occupied a number of different locations in the northwestern part of the state near present-day Kansas City. Constant friction and occasional violence with their neighbors followed. The Missourians proved to be intolerant, but the Mormons also seemed to go out of their way to provoke them. The Mormons, like most religious sects, instinctively sensed that

This sampler, embroidered about 1846, depicts the Latter-day Saints' temple in Nauvoo, Illinois, along with the names of church leaders. Mormons earned distinction for the beauty of their folk art.

opposition toughened the spiritual muscles. And opposition also helped them distinguish loyal partisans from fair-weather friends. But enough was enough. Ten months later Smith and most of his followers moved back eastward to Nauvoo, Illinois, a dusty village on the Mississippi.

Nauvoo thrived—for a while, at least. Thousands of converts, including many won by Mormon missionaries in England, flocked to the settlement, boosting the population to 10,000 by 1840. The Mormons' businesses prospered. Smith received additional revelations, which took the Mormons farther and farther from evangelical Protestantism. For example, Smith received instructions that the Mormons should secure their dead ancestors' places in heaven by baptizing them by name, going back at least four generations (thus accounting for the Mormons' impressive efforts to recover the genealogical history of thousands of U.S. families). In Nauvoo, Smith gradually put into practice his earlier revelation about plural marriage. Whether these were actual or symbolic marriages remains disputed, although solid evidence supports the former. Before long, Smith also established a Mormon militia, declared himself king of the kingdom of God, and announced his intention to run for President of the United States. When an opposition newspaper questioned these moves, the Prophet closed it in the spring of 1844. Then, finding himself in grave trouble, he gave himself up to the law.

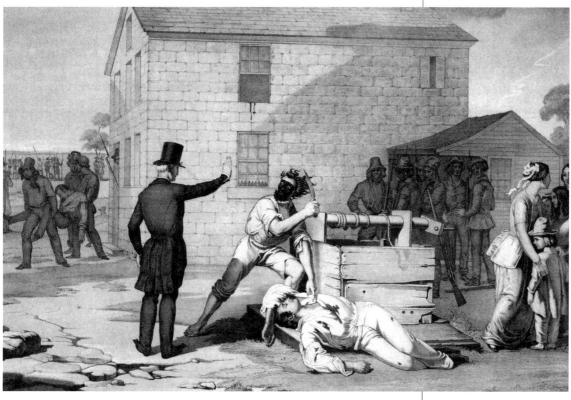

The authorities jailed him and his brother Hyrum in nearby Carthage. On June 27, 1844, a mob broke into the jail and murdered the two brothers in cold blood.

A power struggle ensued. Soon the Mormons chose Brigham Young as president of the church. Like the Smith family, the Young family had migrated in the early 19th century from Vermont to upstate New York to find work. Although Young had been baptized as a Methodist, he remained dissatisfied with the exclusiveness of evangelical Protestantism. In 1832 he embraced the Mormon message. Young was not as charismatic as Smith, but he proved to be a strong leader and a superb organizer. Recognizing that the Gentile culture in Illinois would never tolerate the increasingly distinctive sect in their midst, Young led a contingent westward. Heading out along the Missouri River in the bitter winter of 1846, the first Mormons arrived in Utah's Great Salt Lake Basin 17

Mormons in Illinois antagonized their "Gentile" neighbors, and their neighbors responded with deadly violence. Although the details remain fuzzy, tradition holds that one of Joseph Smith's murderers tried (without success) to behead him.

Brigham Young, the Latter-day Saints' second president, led Joseph Smith's discouraged followers from Illinois to Utah in 1846–47. In Utah, Young governed the church with a benign but iron hand.

months later. When Young initially eyed the awesome valley from the surrounding Wasatch Range, he reportedly declared, with characteristic finality: "This is the place." The Mormons called their newfound home Deseret, a word they coined meaning honeybee. In 1850 Utah organized itself as a territory. In 1852 the practice of plural marriage (which had grown quietly since the Prophet's death in 1844) was openly acknowledged. By the time of Young's death a quarter century later, Mormons had established 350 settlements, numbering 100,000 residents, stretching from Idaho to southern California.

A minority of Mormons, led by Joseph Smith's wife, Emma Hale Smith, and his son Joseph Smith III, never joined the main body in Utah. In 1852 they structured themselves as the Reorganized Church of Jesus Christ of Latter Day Saints (differently punctuated). The Reorganized Mormons, as they called themselves, remained strongest in northern Missouri and southern Iowa, where they established Graceland College. Theologically they came to resemble the restoration-minded Christians/Disciples of Christ.

Gentile visitors to Utah in the latter years of the 19th century encountered a well-ordered, economically prosperous society. An elaborate communal irrigation system helped the Mormons create a garden in the wilderness. Nonetheless, their insistence upon plural marriage sparked repeated confrontations with neighboring Gentiles and the U.S. government. Federal legislation in 1862 prohibiting bigamy was affirmed in a landmark 1879 Supreme Court case, *United States* vs. *Reynolds*. In the face of ever-tightening sanctions by the federal government, not to mention continued outcries among the public back East, the Mormons finally suspended their practice of plural marriage in 1890. This move allowed the Utah Territory to enter the union as a state in 1896. (Mormons today no longer practice plural marriage; those groups who do are not officially recognized by the church.) Although Gentiles commonly assumed that Mormon plural marriage degraded women, Utah guaranteed women the right to vote in 1896, making it only the second state to do so, following Wyoming in 1890. In the late 1990s the Latter-day Saints claimed nearly 10 million adherents worldwide, with half of them living in the United States.

How should we interpret the relationship between the Mormons and the rest of U.S. culture in the 19th century? To some extent the Mormons represented a new religion, one as different from historic Christianity as Christianity was from Judaism. Their tenets of plural marriage, a material

Migrating Mormons trekked across Iowa, Nebraska, and Wyoming, and over the Rocky Mountains into Utah. This wagon train entered Echo Canyon, Utah, in 1867.

God (made of matter, rather than just an idea), and continuing revelation set them apart. So did their insistence upon a centrally planned economy (especially in the 1850s, when they were forced to grapple with the harshness of the Utah desert). At the same time, however, the Mormons' strong sense of personal morality, their optimistic view of human nature, and their conviction that the United States provided the main stage for God's plan for all of human history drew them squarely into the American mainstream. By the end of the 20th century the Mormons had become less recognizable as a distinct culture. Some of their theological beliefs still aroused suspicion among evangelical Christians. Socially, however, the Mormons were patriotic, hardworking, middle-class Americans.

One of the most important things to remember about the Mormons is that they were restorers. They believed that true Christianity had been

Mormon Alvin F. Heaton, his two wives, and their large family pose at Moccasin Springs, Arizona in 1907. The practice of plural marriage, which lasted about 40 years, made Mormons unique among Christians in America.

lost, but God Himself had reinstated it in 19th-century America. They saw themselves not simply copying the ancient Israelites and Christians, but *re-creating* both the Old Testament Israelites and the New Testament Christians in the modern world. It was an exhilarating vision. Little wonder that tens of thousands of Americans, as well as equal numbers in other countries, found Mormonism compelling enough to warrant the long trek to Utah.

School Room.

Chapter 5

Outsiders

Swing low, sweet chariot,
Coming for to carry me home;
Swing low, sweet chariot,
Coming for to carry me home.
I looked over Jordan,
And what did I see,
Coming for to carry me home?
A band of angels coming after me,
Coming for to carry me home.
    —*"Swing Low," African American Spiritual*

Who is an outsider? Sooner or later most people consider themselves outsiders: left out, unappreciated, maybe even despised. For most people these feelings can be written off as the gloomy sentiments that come and go like a rainy day. But not always—sometimes exclusion is very real. In the 19th century millions of Americans found themselves perennial outsiders. Some acquired that status because they held religious beliefs that the rest of the society judged unacceptable. Others experienced exclusion because they belonged to the wrong racial or ethnic group. We should not assume that the groups we shall study were always unhappy. Far from it. Much of the time, and perhaps most of the time, they built meaningful lives despite their forced separation from the rest of American life. Nonetheless, insiders could choose to recognize or not recognize outsiders as they wished. Outsiders never had that option.

The Native Americans were outsiders because of their faith. Their religious traditions stretched back at least 10,000 years, long before the

A Shoshone Indian ritual, the traditional Sun Dance performed to ensure successful buffalo hunting, adorns this 19th-century elk hide. The dancers' orientation to one another and to the Sun Dance center pole, topped with a buffalo head and tail, express the well-being of the society.

oldest parts of the Hebrew Bible were written. Their traditions varied greatly. Those of the Iroquois, the Cherokees, the Sioux, and the Hopis (to name a few of the most prominent) differed as much from each other as those of the Protestants differed from the Roman Catholics'. Nonetheless, the Indian religions of the 19th century shared a number of features. Most notably, sacred threads wove all aspects of life into a single tapestry. It was no more possible to choose one's religion than to choose one's family. Indian beliefs also presupposed the continuity of time. Whereas modern Westerners subdivided time into religious and nonreligious units, so that a person did sacred things on Sunday or Saturday and secular things the rest of the week, the Native Americans knew no such distinctions. To them all time seemed the same.

The continuity of time manifested itself in the various Indian languages, which generally made no clear distinctions between past, present, and future. This dismayed Christian missionaries, who wanted to teach the Indians about the future life. The same held true for space. The Western notion of owning a plot of land was alien to the Indian mind. To be sure, one or another nation might have occupied a given plot of land for hunting or raising crops, and they would fight to protect it. But no one owned land independently of using it. All space, in other words, existed for human as well as animal sustenance.

The Native Americans' notion of God or gods also differed from Western ideas, in quite striking ways. Some Indian nations imagined a distant creator God, but allowed God no active role in the world's affairs. Most groups, however, supposed a wide range of supernatural beings who had helped to create the human race. The creation process needed to be reenacted on a regular basis through dances and the telling and retelling of sacred stories. At the same time, the Indians' cosmos brimmed with supernatural power in the sky, in the trees, in the ground. This force was neither good nor bad in itself. It all depended upon how it was used. Rituals thus emerged in order to help humans use supernatural power for constructive purposes. The shaman or holy man (who was occasionally a holy woman) played a special role too. Either through natural talents or acquired training, the shaman traveled into the supernatural realm, where he received extraordinary powers. These newly received energies allowed him to cure illnesses, interpret dreams, and influence nature.

Although the core beliefs and practices of the Indian traditions remained firmly outside the U.S. religious mainstream, a lot of melding took place at the edges. Christian missionaries to the Indians occasionally embraced an Indian religion, wholly or in part. Both whites and blacks absorbed aspects of Indian myths, mixing their own semi-Christian beliefs in ghosts, witches, demons, and sprites with Native American accounts of similar experiences. For example, Joel Chandler Harris's Uncle Remus tales, published in various forms in the 1880s and 1890s, featured a wise old black man telling stories about Brer Rabbit. As in the Cherokee and Creek legends, Brer Rabbit emerged as a trickster character who could change form at will, confusing his supposedly smart and powerful antagonists.

MISSIONARIES OF THE BUDDHIST FAITH.

Two Representatives of the Ancient Creed Are in San Francisco to Proselyte.

DR. SHUYE SONODA   REV. KAHURYO NISHIJIMA

DR. SHUYE SONODA and Rev. Kahuryo Nishijima, two Buddhist priests, who are the sons of Buddhist priests of Japan, have come here to establish a Buddhist mission at 807 Polk street and to convert Japanese and later Americans to the ancient Buddhist faith. They will teach that God is not the creator, but the created; not a real existence, but a figment of the human imagination, and that pure Buddhism is a better moral guide than Christianity.

Their priestly robes are as interesting as the lessons that they would present. As they posed before the camera in a hallway near their rooms in the Occidental Hotel yesterday they were the wonderment of all the Japanese employes who could assemble for a glimpse of the sacred garb.

Dr. Shuye Sonoda and the Reverend Kahuryo Nishijima were the first Buddhist missionaries to the United States. According to this 1899 *San Francisco Chronicle* article, they came to America to teach that God is "not a real existence, but a figment of the human imagination."

Some Shakers felt that Indian spirits regularly visited them and took possession of their bodies. The list of such cultural exchanges could be extended at length. In the give and take of ordinary life the lines between historic Christianity and non-Christian traditions blurred more than the purists on either side wanted to admit.

Asians also represented outsiders because of their faith. The Chinese started emigrating to the United States during the California gold rush of the 1850s, their numbers soon swelling into the tens of thousands. They brought their religions with them: Buddhism, Taoism, Confucianism, and an array of local beliefs. The Japanese laborers who joined the Chinese in the 1870s also brought their religious traditions with them, including distinctively Japanese forms of Buddhism and Taoism.

Other Asians followed. Just as Christian missionaries sailed westward to Asia in the later decades of the 19th century, so too Buddhist missionaries sailed eastward. They first journeyed to the Hawaiian Islands in the late 1880s, then to the West Coast of the continental U.S. the following decade. The Buddhist missionaries hoped to convert Christians to Buddhism, especially to the form of it known as Jodo Shinshu Pure Land Buddhism, which taught that a Pure Land awaited the faithful upon death. The missionaries also hoped to provide material and spiritual support for Japanese workers, most of whom were male, far from home, desperately lonely, and often seeking moral roots.

By the end of the century, sites for the practice of non-Western religions (including centers for Hindus from India and Baha'is from Persia) started popping up on the West Coast and in major cities elsewhere. The Pure Land Buddhists organized themselves in 1899 as the Buddhist Churches of America. Buddhism proved particularly appealing to American intellectuals because of its high ethical ideals. At the World's Parliament of Religions in Chicago in 1893 (part of the World's Columbian

Exposition) some adventurous thinkers even tried to blend Buddhist and Christian teachings. Traditionalists on both sides of the religious fence worried about this mixing and matching of ancient faiths, but there was no going back—as the freewheeling religious marketplace of the late 20th century has amply shown.

Jews too became outsiders of faith. To say that the Jews were marginalized because of their faith is perhaps only partly true, since Judaism formed the basis of Christianity. And in the course of the 19th century Jews moved from being a rarely seen minority to a conspicuous presence on the U.S. cultural landscape, especially in the urban Northeast. Yet the Jews remained distinct from the Christian majority. They did not eat some common foods such as ham or shrimp, they circumcised their male children, and they worshiped on Saturday, which they regarded as the true sabbath. Unlike their Christian neighbors, who based their faith upon both the Old and New Testaments, Jews based theirs upon the Hebrew scriptures (the Old Testament) alone. Jews also esteemed the Talmud, a set of ancient books that interpreted the Hebrew scriptures. Most importantly, the Jews saw themselves as a people specially chosen by God to serve as the bearers of God's laws, including the Ten Commandments, to the rest of the world. The Jews represented the oldest recorded, continuously practiced religious tradition on the North American continent.

The Jewish story in America started long before the Revolutionary War. A handful of Spanish-speaking believers emigrated from Brazil to Rhode Island; Savannah, Georgia; and Charleston, South Carolina, in the 17th century. In the 1820s German-speaking Jews started coming over in large numbers. They soon overwhelmed their Spanish forerunners. The German Jews found work as peddlers, artisans, and shopkeepers in many parts of the country, ranging from Charleston to New York to San Francisco. Many became prosperous and some, such as Judah P. Benjamin, a Confederate cabinet member, quite prominent.

The 1850s marked a watershed in the story of U.S. Judaism. A new and in some ways distinctively American form of the faith then started to crystallize. Its partisans called it Reform Judaism, because they hoped to

THE ISRAELITE.

A weekly Periodical, devoted to the Religion, History and Literature of the Israelites.

PUBLISHED BY

CHAS. F. SCHMIDT & CO.

OFFICE:

NO. 21, EAST THIRD STREET.

"LET THERE BE LIGHT"

EDITED BY

ISAAC MAYER WISE.

RESIDENCE:

NO. 141, EAST THIRD STREET.

Vol. I.   Cincinnati, O., July 28, 5614 A. M., 1854 A. C.   No. 3.

(Continued from No. 2.)

THE CONVERT.

Chapter III.

see their son again. I shall see mine no more." This last remark of Hannah fell heavily upon the members of the family, none of them spoke for a long time. Ra- tongue; then she said in a firm and resolute tone, "Aaron Mast, I am not your intend- ed bride, nor shall I go with you to any place." Zodek advanced towards her, knowing what to make of it; she finally sat down at the table, and leaning her head upon her arms fell asleep. The an- gel of dreams recompensed her richly for

The Israelite, later renamed The American Israelite, was a weekly newspaper edited by Reform rabbi Isaac Mayer Wise. Wise used the paper as a tool to Americanize Judaism.

reform ancient ways and make them more compatible with modern life. Isaac Mayer Wise's long career represented those forces of change well. This eloquent, dynamic Cincinnati rabbi embraced the European Enlightenment of the previous century. Enlightened thinkers had underscored the power of reason to unlock nature's secrets and guide history in the direction of progress. Wise thus called for the orderly worship of an orderly God, preaching and singing in English rather than Hebrew, and for mixed seating, with men and women sitting together. More importantly, Wise departed from the ancient, nearly universal, Jewish conviction that the Messiah would be an actual person. Rather, the Messiah equaled the Jewish religion itself, especially when that religion embodied high ideals like justice, democracy, service to humankind, and the thoughtful worship of God. Wise cemented his ideas in brick. In 1875 he founded Hebrew Union College in Cincinnati, which grew into a leading university in the 20th century.

Predictably, Reform Judaism provoked a reaction. The kind of faith that Wise promoted—urbane, reasonable, and comfortable with middle-class American values—was sharply challenged in the 1880s and 1890s. In those years wave after wave of Jews emigrated from eastern European countries, especially Russia, Poland, Hungary, and Austria. These newcomers

Rabbi Wise Speaks of the Necessity of Change

Isaac Mayer Wise, one of the most prominent and controversial rabbis of the 19th century, urged Jews to accommodate themselves both to American ways and to the most advanced thinking of the age. In this 1871 speech Wise argued that the willingness to embrace change constituted the essence of Reform Judaism in America.

Change, universal and perpetual, is the law of laws in this universe. Still there is an element of stability, the fact of mutation itself; the law of change changes not. . . . Wisdom, boundless and ineffable, and the revelations of Deity lie in this law of laws. . . .

As an illustration of this, it is to be remembered that the Israelite of the reformed school does not believe in the restoration of the ancient mode of worship by the sacrifice of animal victims by a hereditary priesthood. He considers that phase was necessary and beneficial, in its time and locality, but that it would be void of all significance in our age when entirely different conceptions of divine worship prevail, and it would appear much more meaningless to coming generations. The divine institutions of the past are not obligatory on the present generation or on coming ages, because the conditions that rendered them necessary, desirable and beneficial have been radically changed. Therefore, Progressive Judaism [might] be a better designation than Reformed Judaism.

proved to be different from the German Jews in several respects. They were poorer, unskilled, and spoke languages few Americans understood (or wanted to make the effort to understand). Unlike the urbane Germans, these newcomers came from farms and isolated villages in the Old World. In the United States simple survival demanded struggle. As a result, they clustered together for protection in the cities of the urban

Northeast, especially in New York. Most found their lot in the New World extremely hard, even when they were fortunate enough to land a job working for their German brethren. They probably did not possess much sense of ethnic identity before they came, but once here and being reminded daily how different they were, this sense mushroomed.

The newer eastern European Jews proved different from the older German ones in another respect. Simply stated, in matters of religion they often moved to one of two extremes. A minority gave up religion altogether and dubbed themselves freethinkers—free, that is, from the shackles of belief. The majority, in contrast, clung tenaciously to the worship patterns they had nurtured for centuries in the Old World. This meant worshiping and singing in Hebrew, with the men and women sitting apart. It meant that the father exercised control over most aspects of the family's life. And it meant following, as far as possible, all 613 laws prescribed in the Torah, the first five books of Hebrew scripture. By the end of the century these eastern European Jews realized that they needed to organize, partly to distinguish themselves from the Reform Jews, but partly also to protect their beliefs and customs from evaporating in the religious gales of the New World. So they started calling themselves Orthodox Jews. Like numerous Christian bodies, the Orthodox founded schools (notably Yeshiva University in New York City) to preserve their faith among their children and grandchildren.

Not everyone liked these choices, however. For many, Reform Judaism was too liberal, Orthodox Judaism too traditional. Thus, a third major group emerged near the end of the 19th century. They called themselves Conservatives, because they hoped to conserve the best of the past without being enslaved by it. The Conservative Jews believed, for example, that the larger principles encoded in the laws of the Hebrew scriptures remained binding upon modern Jews, but felt that those laws did not have to be followed literally in every respect. The Conservatives also strongly valued the nonreligious aspects of the Jewish heritage, including Jewish literature, drama, music, and cuisine. They too founded schools, most notably Jewish Theological Seminary in New York.

Workers at the Boston Matzo Baking Company sat for this 1894 photograph. In the late 19th century, anti-Semitism began to increase, in large part because of the economic success of some Jews.

By the beginning of the 20th century, then, Jews in America had arrayed themselves in three definable groups that looked very much like those of the Protestant denominations: Reform on the left, Orthodox on the right, and Conservative in the middle. To be sure, the Jews suffered discrimination at the hands of the Protestant majority, especially in clubs and private colleges, but less so than did the Catholics. Unlike the Catholics, the Jews remained too scarce to be perceived as a serious threat. Christians admired Jews' industriousness and their disinclination to seek government help. Besides, millions of Americans fancied themselves a biblical people, extended from the Old Testament Israelites as much as from the New Testament Christians. No wonder that Jews found the United States a congenial home, despite its hardships. For most, Emma Lazarus's timeless words chiseled on the Statue of Liberty rang true: "Give me your tired, your poor, your huddled masses yearning to breathe free."

Yet Lazarus spoke for some more than others. Throughout the 19th century, African Americans remained outsiders in the harshest sense of the term, chained to that status by centuries of custom and statutory law.

More blacks embraced Christianity than any other single religious tradition, yet commonalities of faith proved to be less important than differences of skin color. At the beginning of the century 1 million blacks lived in the United States. Some 90 percent were enslaved, and many lived in the South. By 1860 the black population had swollen to 4 million. Again 90 percent were enslaved, but by then almost all lived in the South. That much is clear. Tracking the slaves' religious progress is considerably more complicated, however.

Bondsmen (as slaves were commonly called) adopted Christianity only slowly. In the 18th century their masters frequently prevented missionaries from contacting the black laborers under their charge lest the Christian message of equality before God make them rebellious. And when missionaries did make contact, they usually met little success. They expected slaves to master lengthy creeds by rote memorization, since slaves could not read and in most places were forbidden by law or custom from learning to do so. Moreover, the church's formal liturgy, or its prescribed pattern of worship, seemed stiff and unnatural to souls accustomed to worshiping in more informal ways. Most damaging of all was that the Church of England's missionaries not only identified themselves with the masters but went out of their way to stress that the Bible taught slaves to be obedient.

The Revolutionary years of the 1770s and 1780s introduced dramatic change as upstart Baptist and Methodist preachers elbowed aside the established Church of England missionaries. The evangelical spokesmen asked no one's permission to preach to the slaves, and success followed. For one thing, they emphasized emotional, heartfelt conversion over the memorization of creeds. They talked about moral accountability—for masters and slaves alike. And they taught that slavery itself was wrong, a sin in God's eyes. This last claim, that slavery was a sin, was one they could not continue to make. By the 1830s evangelical preachers, especially in the South, had lost the will to denounce the "peculiar institution," as southerners called it, for a variety of reasons. One of the most important was the swelling desire for respectability in the eyes of the vaguely Christian majority that endorsed slaveholding. Another involved the growing conviction that all workable societies needed a permanent class of menial laborers in order to survive. Yet the basic principles of evangelical Christianity had already taken firm root and would flourish in the slave community, especially the sense of the equality of all before God. The number of slaves who embraced Christianity is impossible to know, but that they were a large minority seems likely.

Between the Revolution and the Civil War, Christianity took a number of different forms among bondsmen. Most often, perhaps, African Americans worshiped with whites in white-run Baptist and Methodist churches. To say that all worshiped together is not to say that all distinctions faded away, however. Blacks normally sat apart or even in the balcony. And white preachers normally directed words about obedience specifically at them. Even so, whites and blacks heard the same sermon together. They sang and took Holy Communion together. They participated in church disciplinary meetings, not always as equals, but together. And at life's end they were buried in the church cemetery together. Flawed though the system was, Christian worship melded the races as they were nowhere else in southern society.

From time to time African Americans worshiped independently of whites, a pattern that defined a second distinct form of black Christianity. Despite great odds, slaves managed to put up meetinghouses of their own. The Silver Bluff Baptist Church in South Carolina offers a prominent example. There, numerous black preachers gained fame for their ability to move whites as well as their own people to tearful conversions. By the 1840s, however, independent black worship of this sort had fallen into decline. On at least three occasions Christian teachings had been used by fiery black prophets to justify slave insurrections: Gabriel Prosser's uprising in Richmond, Virginia, in 1800; Denmark Vesey's in Charleston, South Carolina, in 1822; and Nat Turner's in Southampton County, Virginia, in 1831. For these and other reasons, white authorities increasingly cracked down on any signs of black independence, including unsupervised worship.

And then there was the Invisible Institution, called invisible because it took place outside whites' vision. As the planters' oversight of slave life grew more oppressive, African Americans responded by praising God in their huts, in forested meadows, or simply in the dark of night—anyplace, in short, where whites could not see. In those settings black preachers delivered God's word freely, often in memorized phrases that evoked powerful images of past bondage and future liberation, both physical and spiritual. They spoke especially of Moses leading his people across the Red Sea to freedom, and of the lowly Jesus suffering for the sins of others.

In those unseen meetings the slaves experienced assurance of their worth in God's eyes, as well as the resources for bringing moral discipline to their lives and, by force of example, to their masters' lives. Those settings also moved the slaves to create a distinctive form of song, the spiritual. This type of music combined lyrics and tunes common in white evangelical circles with ones of their own creation. "Swing Low, Sweet Chariot" and "Joshua Fit de Battle of Jericho," at once powerfully rhythmic and melancholy, ranked among the timeless favorites.

Evangelical Protestantism by no means commanded the loyalty of all slaves, however. For one thing, probably a majority of African Americans, like a majority of whites, remained outside the reach of the church. Also, Roman Catholic missionaries won a small minority of followers, especially in Louisiana and Maryland. And finally, some blacks retained the religious traditions of their native West Africa. One of the most visible examples was voodoo, or Vodun, an import from Africa and Haiti that focused upon the healing powers in certain herbs and plant roots.

Before the Civil War most African Americans lived in the South as slaves, but about 10 percent resided in the North, sometimes enslaved but sometimes free, as slavery slowly died out in the North between the Revolution and the Civil War. Northern blacks scattered themselves along the whole spectrum of Protestant denominations. Shortly after the Revolution, however, the seeds of two independent black denominations were sown: the African Methodist Episcopal Church (commonly called the A.M.E. Church), and the similar African Methodist Episcopal Zion Church (commonly called the A.M.E.Z. Church).

Both groups claimed urban origins. The story of the A.M.E. began with Richard Allen. Born a slave in Philadelphia in 1760, Allen converted

to Methodism as a teenager and entered the ministry. Clearly he had found his calling, for soon afterward Allen's master also converted and allowed him to purchase his freedom. The young evangelist preached in the Philadelphia area, eventually making that city's St. George's Methodist Church his church home. For a while things went well, but the growing presence of African Americans at St. George's eventually aroused whites' fears. One Sunday morning (probably in 1787) some white trustees yanked a prominent black man to his feet because he was kneeling in an area reserved for whites. Outraged, Allen determined never to return. In 1794 he opened Bethel Church for Negro Methodists, probably the first regular black church meeting in the United States. Bethel evolved into the A.M.E. in 1816. A similar train of events, augmented by rivalry for scarce resources within the black community, prompted the formation of the A.M.E.Z. in New York in 1821. Although both groups prospered after the Civil War by attending to both the material and spiritual needs of their

A commemorative engraving produced by the African Methodist Episcopal Church in 1876 depicts Richard Allen, founder of the church, surrounded by 10 other bishops. The corner scenes depict various A.M.E.-sponsored institutions, including Wilberforce University in Ohio, which was founded in 1856.

people, the A.M.E. in particular gravitated toward structured worship and middle-class respectability.

Following the Civil War, African Americans established additional groups. After several false starts they organized the National Baptist Convention in Atlanta in 1895. This body soon became the largest black denomination in the United States. Regional pride played a powerful role for blacks, just as it did for whites. The Colored (now Christian) Methodist Episcopal Church established itself in 1870 to provide a home for southern black Methodists who did not feel at home in either of the northern A.M.E. churches, because of the churches' growing respectability and Yankee flavor, or in the mostly white Methodist Episcopal Church, South. At the very end of the century a group of fervent evangelicals in Mississippi and Tennessee coalesced in a loose fellowship called the Church of God in Christ. This body endorsed divine healing and, by 1907, speaking in tongues (a kind of rapid, involuntary speech that always souded like a foreign language). Both healing and tongues formed hallmarks of the emerging Pentecostal movement.

By the end of the century probably about half of the African Americans in the United States considered themselves Christians in a self-

A large crowd gathers to watch people being baptized in a spring in Huntsville, Alabama. Outdoor, public baptisms were typical of African-American churches in the South.

conscious way, and nearly all in a broadly cultural way. The great majority, in any event, were affiliated with Baptist or Methodist bodies. Most of the rest were Catholics living in Louisiana. Nineteenth-century blacks also fashioned hundreds of quasi-religious brotherhoods and sisterhoods for recreation, fellowship, and mutual help. Well-known examples included the Prince Hall Masons and the Colored Oddfellows.

The African-American church served as a center for many aspects of life. Excluded from white-run schools, businesses, and churches, blacks created a separate world of their own inside the limits of their churches. Those settings offered ambitious and talented young men a place to display their abilities. Black groups rarely ordained women, but females— affectionately dubbed "Mothers of the Church"—routinely shouldered the hard, day-to-day work of visiting the sick and teaching the young. Women also exercised powerful leadership roles in informal ways. Male ministers ignored them at their peril. Beyond all this, many (although certainly not all) black churches retained the worship patterns of the antebellum years, emphasizing clapping, enthusiastic singing, and a call-and-response style of preaching.

In the latter part of the 19th century many of these currents flowed together in the life of Amanda Berry Smith. Born a slave in 1837, Smith knew that God had called her to the ministry. Unable to receive ordination because of her sex, Smith nonetheless launched out on her own as an independent evangelist in the Wesleyan tradition. Thousands professed conversion under her ministry. Smith gave the word energetic new dimensions of meaning. She traveled to England in 1878, to India in 1879, to Liberia in 1881, back to England in 1889, and finally settled in Chicago in 1892. She started a home for orphans near there in 1899. Outsiders smirked, saying that leaders like Smith offered pie-in-the-sky rewards in heaven rather than real-life ones in the here and now. But she knew they were wrong—as did millions of others—for the old-time religion met enduring needs of the human spirit in the trials and tribulations of the present.

Evangelical preacher Amanda Smith wrote in her autobiography, "Our house was one of the main stations of the Under Ground Railroad. After working all day in the harvest field, [my father] would come home at night, sleep about two hours, then start at midnight and walk fifteen or twenty miles and carry a poor slave to a place of security."

Chapter 6

Warriors

Mine eyes have seen the glory
of the coming of the Lord;
He is trampling out the vintage
where the grapes of wrath are stored;
He hath loosed the fateful lightning
of his terrible swift sword;
His truth is marching on.
    —*Julia Ward Howe, "Battle Hymn of the Republic" (1861)*

President Abraham Lincoln (center) with two Union Army officers at Antietam, Maryland, in 1862. In an address after the Civil War had ended, Lincoln proclaimed that God had allowed the war in order to punish both sides for allowing slavery to exist.

t proved to be the costliest war in American history. Six hundred thousand died, and another million fell as casualties. All the wars that the United States fought combined—from the Revolution through Vietnam—totaled fewer deaths than the Civil War. Besides unprecedented destruction, the Civil War (or the War between the States, as it was, and still is, commonly called in the South) harbored many ironies. More died of disease than of gunshot wounds. Early in the conflict President Abraham Lincoln asked Colonel Robert E. Lee of Virginia to lead the Union army (Lee would ultimately lead the *Confederate* forces). Four of Lincoln's brothers-in-law would fight for the South, and one would die in the Rebel cause.

Religion accounted for many of the deepest ironies. Some of the bloodiest battles ever fought on the North American continent, including Shiloh and Antietam, were waged in the front yards of country churches. The Battle of Gettysburg, by some accounts the grisliest of all, unfolded on the outskirts of a Lutheran seminary campus. Christian pastors on both sides of the Mason-Dixon line incited conflict by their unwillingness to compromise. And once the fighting started, they intensified its ferocity by invoking the fires of divine sanction (the idea that God supported one or the other side in the conflict). When the bloodshed stopped, they perpetuated ill feelings for years by their unapologetic defense of their own side's cause.

Religious beliefs fed the ideologies that fed the war. Elijah P. Lovejoy, a Presbyterian minister turned newspaper editor, offers a case in point. When this Maine-born, Princeton-educated pastor first opened his printing press in St. Louis, he seemed mostly concerned to attack Catholics, Baptists, and members of the Disciples of Christ. But the sin of human bondage gnawed at his conscience. By the 1830s Lovejoy had moved across the river to Alton, Illinois, and pitted himself unalterably against slavery. Convinced that slaveowners routinely raped their female slaves, among other evils, Lovejoy devoted himself to the cause of immediate abolition. Mobs destroyed his press three times and in 1837 they took his life as well.

For Southerners too, religion and politics merged. Exactly 25 years after Lovejoy's death Leonidas Polk, Episcopal bishop of Louisiana, heard his region's call. Polk promptly exchanged his bishop's robes for the uniform of a Confederate major general. In years past he had devoted his efforts to the conversion and religious instruction of slaves, winning respect for humane treatment of the hundreds of bondsmen he himself had owned. But now it was time to fight, and fight he did, with brilliance and valor, until the summer of 1864, when a cannonball claimed his life in the Battle of Atlanta.

Where religious conviction ended and outright fanaticism began was sometimes hard to say. Two of the men who did the most to stir up undying hatred, Northerner John Brown and Southerner John Wilkes Booth, both felt that they had been called by God to carry out their bloody tasks. Brown, a radical Presbyterian, not only believed that slavery was wrong but also that God had called him to start a war that would smash the slaveholding system. In the 1850s this avenger journeyed to Kansas, where he murdered five pro-slavery sympathizers in cold blood. He then moved

on to Harpers Ferry, Virginia (now West Virginia), where he tried to spark a nationwide slave insurrection by taking over a federal arsenal. Brown went to the gallows on December 2, 1859, convinced that he had served his nation and his God well.

The same pattern held true for stage actor John Wilkes Booth, who had hurried from Richmond to Harpers Ferry to witness Brown's execution. Though Booth never possessed the courage actually to enlist in the Confederate army, he felt that God had called him to execute the President who had plunged his beloved South into smoking ruins. Thus, on April 14, 1865, he slipped into Ford's Theater in Washington, D.C., and shot Lincoln point blank in the back of the head. Booth too met violent death—his turn came 12 days later—convinced that he had obeyed the plain instructions of his conscience and his Lord.

The Civil War stemmed from many causes. Dramatically different notions about what a United States of America really meant played a large

Illinois editor Elijah Love-joy saw his printing press wrecked and his warehouse destroyed because of his abolitionist views. Lovejoy was not the first—nor the last—American to discover that free speech came dear. A mob took his life in 1837.

John Steuart Curry's 20th-century mural of John Brown, *Tragic Prelude,* in the Kansas State Capitol, evoked the image of an Old Testament prophet gone mad.

role. Indeed, until the mid-19th century many Americans, especially Southerners, customarily used a plural verb when speaking of the nation ("the United States are . . ."). After all, what came first, the federal Constitution or the rights of the individual states? Growing sectional rivalry contributed to the bitterness as well. Nonetheless, most historians believe that the question of black servitude remained the primary cause of the war. The problem of course was that the Constitution guaranteed the states' right to practice slavery if they wished. The slave trade ended in 1808, but not the practice. The number of bondsmen had grown from 400,000 at the time the Constitution was ratified in 1791 to 3.5 million on the eve of the Civil War. Although Northerners had long profited from the goods that Southerners produced with slave labor, the Northern states had gradually abolished the system. Slavery remained the South's peculiar problem.

White Christian opposition to slavery began nearly a century before the Civil War. Although a few Puritans and many Quakers had spoken out against the practice since the early 18th century, serious opposition to it began in 1784 when the Methodist Church prohibited both clergy and lay persons from holding slaves. The Baptists and Quakers instituted similar measures in the same period, both in the North and the South. As late as 1818 the General Assembly of the Presbyterian Church declared slavery a "gross violation of human nature" and called Christians to erase it as speedily as possible. Although all these admonitions received mixed enforcement, the principle remained clear.

Gradually, however, opposition to slavery localized in the states north of the Mason-Dixon line. Much, and perhaps most, of the antislavery sentiment stemmed from religious impulses. The year 1819 saw the formation of the American Colonization Society, which sought to buy slaves and send them back to Africa. Several thousand went, forming the nation of Liberia. Although later generations viewed this recolonization scheme as impractical at best and racist at worst, at the time many thousands of Christians, both white and black, deemed it a reasonable solution to an unreasonable problem.

By the 1830s millions of Christians, mostly in the North, were pressing for the abolition of the "peculiar institution." Some wanted all the slaves freed immediately, with little regard for the economic consequences for owners or to the slaves themselves. William Lloyd Garrison, a Boston journalist, emerged as one of the most outspoken representatives of this approach, commonly called immediatism. Once influenced by the Quakers, this fiery New Englander found himself increasingly alienated from all forms of orthodox Christianity. Nonetheless, his conscience burned brightly. In 1831 Garrison launched a radical paper called the *Liberator*. His speeches and articles stirred evangelicals and non-evangelicals

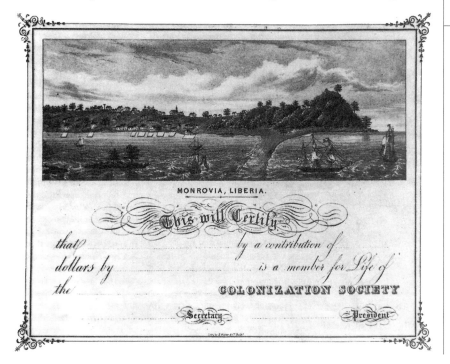

MONROVIA, LIBERIA.

This will Certify

that _____ *by a contribution of* _____

dollars by _____ *is a member for Life of*

the _____ COLONIZATION SOCIETY

Secretary _____ *President*

This romanticized sketch of the Liberian capital of Monrovia on a certificate of contribution suggested freedom from want as well as from white ownership. For thousands of enslaved blacks, the idea of making a new life for themselves in a new African country shone as a wondrous hope.

FIFTH ANNIVERSARY
OF THE
MASSACHUSETTS ANTI-SLAVERY SOCIETY,
WEDNESDAY, JANUARY 25, 1837.

[☞ The public meetings, during the day, will be held in the SPACIOUS LOFT, OVER THE STABLE OF THE MARLBOROUGH HOTEL, and in the evening, in the REPRESENTATIVES' HALL.]

HOURS OF THE MEETINGS.

Meeting for Delegates at 9 o'clock in the morning, at 46, Washington-Street.

First public meeting at 10 o'clock A. M., in the LOFT OVER THE STABLE OF THE MARLBOROUGH HOTEL.

Second public meeting at 1-2 past 2 o'clock, P. M. same place.

Evening meeting at 1-2 past 6 o'clock, in the REPRESENTATIVES' HALL.

☞ The Committee of Arrangements respectfully inform the ladies that ample accommodations have been prepared for them. The loft is spacious, clean, well warmed, and will accommodate, with ease and perfect safety, at least 1000 persons.

☞ AMOS DRESSER, a citizen of this State, who was 'Lynched' at Nashville, for the crime of being an Abolitionist, will be present, and during the meetings in the afternoon and evening, will give a history of that affair.

By virtue of special compact, Shylock demanded a pound of flesh, cut nearest to the heart. Those who sell mothers separately from their children, likewise claim a legal right to human flesh; and they too cut it nearest to the *heart.—L. M. Child.*

On, woman! from thy happy hearth
Extend thy gentle hand to save
The poor and perishing of earth—
The chained and stricken slave!
Oh, plead for all the suffering of thy kind—
For the crushed body and the darkened
mind. *J. G. Whittier.*

Anti-slavery societies often ran revival-like meetings. They called people to come, to repent of the sin of slavery, and then to go forth with a renewed sense of the need to work for reform.

alike to form antislavery societies. Garrison's constant agitation not only raised Northerners' awareness of the cruelties of slavery but also helped characterize the system as sinful. The evil of slavery so incensed Garrison that he soon urged the *North* to secede from the Union lest it soil itself by association with the South.

For most Northerners, immediate abolition seemed impractical. They opted instead for step-by-step elimination of the slave system—an approach commonly called gradualism—either by halting its spread into the territories of the West or by compensating slaveowners for loss of their "property." Many of these reformers had been converted to evangelical Christianity during the revivals of the Second Great Awakening. For example, the revivalist Charles G. Finney forthrightly defined slavery as sinful. Because the Constitution guaranteed the legality of slavery, Finney urged Christians to do the next best thing: mount moral pressure against the system in every way possible. Although he saw no way to make slavery illegal, he wanted to make it unthinkable.

Many evangelicals fell somewhere between Garrison's desire for immediate abolition and Finney's willingness to accept gradual abolition. Consider, for instance, the career of Theodore Dwight Weld, one of Finney's most energetic converts. This young firebrand was expelled from the Presbyterians' Lane Theological Seminary in Cincinnati, where he was a student, for preaching against slavery and for associating with blacks as friends. Weld and a group of supporters, known as the Lane Rebels, then moved to the infant Oberlin College, near Cleveland. In time they formed influential networks of friendship and communication, and Weld himself later married the prominent abolitionist and women's rights advocate Angelina Grimke. Many secular abolitionists were driven by principles of universal brotherhood and sisterhood, derived from the mid-century democratic and humanitarian revolutions going on in Europe. In contrast, evangelicals like the Lane Rebels acted from a biblical notion of humans' equality before God, as well as a conviction that the United States could never become God's land until Christians purged the sin of slavery from their midst.

Orator Frederick Douglass exposed the hypocrisy of white Christianity as incisively as any. Born a slave in Maryland about 1817, Douglass taught himself to read by poring over the Bible. He escaped to Massachusetts in 1838. Once free, he championed the causes of temperance, women's rights, and, above all, antislavery. In his autobiography (published in 1845 as *Narrative of the Life of Frederick Douglass*), the former slave argued that a canyon separated the false religion of the slaveholder from the true religion of Christ. In the former, Douglass declared, the man who wielded the "blood clotted" whip during the week stood behind the sacred pulpit on Sunday. The man who robbed the slave of his earnings presumed to teach him the Bible. The man who stole the slave's sister and sold her into prostitution presented himself as an "advocate of purity." The man who tore wives from husbands and children from their parents in order to turn a profit preached about the wholesomeness of families. In

Christianity and the Slaveholding Religion

In the Narrative of the Life of Frederick Douglass *(1845), this eloquent former slave distinguished authentic Christianity from the vicious, corrupted form of that religion that pervaded the South and legitimized the slave system. Douglass's anger about the hypocrisy of slave Christianity was shared by many whites as well as blacks and helped to spark the Civil War.*

This daguerrotype of Frederick Douglass in his 20s may be the earliest portrait of the orator. By the end of his life in 1895, Douglass probably ranked as the best-known African-American Christian in the United States.

What I have said respecting and against religion, I mean strictly to apply to the *slaveholding religion* of this land, and with no possible reference to Christianity proper; for, between the Christianity of this land, and the Christianity of Christ, I recognize the widest possible difference—so wide, that to receive the one as good, pure, and holy, is of necessity to reject the other as bad, corrupt, and wicked. To be the friend of the one, is of necessity to be the enemy of the other. I love the pure, peaceable, and impartial Christianity of Christ: I therefore hate the corrupt, slaveholding, women-whipping, cradle-plundering, partial and hypocritical Christianity of this land. . . . [R]evivals of religion and revivals in the slave-trade go hand in hand together. The slave prison and the church stand near each other. The clanking of fetters and the rattling of chains in the prison, and the pious psalm and solemn prayer in the church, may be heard at the same time. Dealers in the bodies and souls of men erect their stand in the presence of the pulpit, and they mutually help each other. The dealer gives his blood-stained gold to support the pulpit, and the pulpit, in return, covers his infernal business with the garb of Christianity. Here we have religion and robbery the allies of each other—devils dressed in angels' robes, and hell presenting the semblance of paradise.

sum, Douglass proclaimed with right-eous indignation, "[We] have men-stealers for ministers, women-whippers for missionaries, and cradle-plunderers for church members."

One religiously inspired woman, Harriet Beecher Stowe, may have done more to undermine slavery than any other single person. Stowe's Christian credentials ran deep. Her father, Lyman Beecher, was a well-known Presbyterian theologian and seminary president in Ohio. He strongly disliked slavery and said so. Stowe herself won lasting fame for her novel *Uncle Tom's Cabin,* which was published in 1852 and frequently republished and, more importantly per-haps, turned into a long-running New York play. The novel told the story of a God-fearing slave family, ruthlessly broken up by traders who bought and sold the laborers as if they were nothing but horses. Although the novel bordered upon allegory, with most of the characters overdrawn as either entirely evil or entirely good, it powerfully stirred the Northern conscience against the brutality and un-Christian character of the slave system.

The characters Uncle Tom and Topsy appeared in these posters advertising the popular New York play adapted from Harriet Beecher Stowe's *Uncle Tom's Cabin.* Like Stowe's book, the show had some-what unrealistic charac-ters, but it did bring the evils of slavery to wide public attention.

Southern Christians took none of this agitation lying down. They mounted a fierce defense of their way of life. As far back as the 1640s, the Church of England (later the Episcopal Church) in Virginia had stated unequivocally that slavery remained compatible with Christianity. For the 60 years or so from the 1760s through the 1820s the Methodists and Bap-tists in the South had opposed slavery. They considered it sinful and associated it with elite plantation owners whom they strongly disliked anyway. But by the second third of the 19th century most Southern Christians, including the Methodists and Baptists, had changed their minds: maybe slavery was not so sinful after all.

Slavery's advocates offered several reasons. They typically began by noting that the Old Testament patriarchs owned slaves and the New Testament did not condemn them for it. Indeed, the New Testament urged slaves to be obedient to their masters. In the Book of Philemon, for example, Saint Paul himself urges a runaway slave to return to his owner. (Southern and Northern Protestants looked to the same Bible, but the former tended to interpret it literally, the latter figuratively.) Southerners added that most slaves would have remained ignorant of Christianity if they had been left in Africa, where their immortal souls would have perished in hell. Southern Christians also argued that the slavery system compared favorably with the inhuman working conditions in the mines and factories of the North. Above all, they believed that the slave system embodied a reasonable way to organize a society, especially if the slaves were Christianized and treated as fully human children rather than as less-than-human brutes.

Given such enormous differences in outlook between the regions, by the mid-1840s millions of men and women on both sides of the Mason-Dixon line had come to believe that the separation of the North and South was inevitable. And so it was that the churches embarked upon the road to war.

The largest Protestant sects led the way. First came the Presbyterians, who split into "new school" and "old school" factions in 1837. This rupture primarily involved other issues, such as whether humans had any ability to embrace Christ on their own (the new schoolers said yes, the old schoolers no). The new school split along sectional lines in 1857, the old school in 1861. Next came the Methodists, the largest Protestant denomination and one of the largest organizations of any kind in the nation. In 1843 a sizable bloc in New York state broke from the Methodist Church, because they felt the church was too timid about condemning slavery. This faction called themselves Wesleyan Methodists, partly to underscore John Wesley's own opposition to slavery. In 1844 things came to a head among the main body of Methodists when a Georgia bishop acquired slaves through marriage. When the General Conference of the Methodist

Church demanded his resignation, the Southern Methodists walked out. They formed their own body the following year, labeling it the Methodist Episcopal Church, South. Similar resentments triggered the separation of Northern and Southern Baptists in 1845. For the Baptists the question was whether missionaries could own slaves. When it became clear that Northerners, who controlled the Baptist missionary agencies, would no longer endorse having slave-owning missionaries, the Southerners set up their own group, the Southern Baptist Convention.

All these animosities ran deep. The Northern and Southern Methodists did not reunite until 1939 (and the black Methodists were effectively kept out until 1958), the Presbyterians did not come together again until 1983, and the Northern and Southern Baptists have never reunited.

Among the other main religious groups, the northern and southern Roman Catholic churches broke apart when the nation did in 1861, but readily reunited at war's end, partly because they owed final religious allegiance to the church in Rome, not to any one region of a nation. The Episcopalians followed a similar pattern of splitting and reuniting as the nation did. Most of the remaining Christian bodies did not officially separate, but that was not because of tender feelings for one another. Some, such as the Unitarians and Congregationalists, were already concentrated in the northern section of the country. Others, like the Disciples of Christ, proved too locally based to break apart. The Lutherans were too preoccupied with their own ethnic and doctrinal concerns to focus on separating. The same held true for the Jews.

But the largest denominations had fractured, one by one. And when they did, Americans of all persuasions resigned themselves to the inevitability of war. A Presbyterian preacher said in 1837 that the Potomac River would be "dyed with blood." Seven years later a Methodist clergyman predicted that the "fiercest passions" of human nature would soon be arrayed against each other. If Christians who shared so much could not work things out, how could others expect to be successful?

When the fighting actually erupted in the green fields of Virginia in the spring of 1861, religious men—and not a few women—rushed to do their share, and perhaps a bit more than their share. Ministers on both sides rallied partisans to fight for their cause and their region. Northern clergy argued that the sin of slavery would have to be purged before the millennium (the thousand years of peace and prosperity the Bible promised) could dawn. Southern clergy countered that the North was the land of infidelity, the South the land of faithfulness to biblical ideals. God had, they said, specially chosen the South to show the world what a truly Christian society looked like. Indeed, the Constitution of the Confederate States of America (unlike that of the United States) explicitly identified the Confederacy as a Christian nation.

As the fighting dragged on, Christian organizations on both sides supplied spiritual and material comfort. Northern churches provided hundreds of chaplains and relief workers to the war effort. Scores of women served as nurses. The American Red Cross had its beginnings in the Sanitary Commission, a Unitarian effort to care for the wounded and dying. By the same token, Southern armies saw wave after wave of revival fervor. Some Southern chaplains even promised young Rebels that they would go directly to heaven if they were slain on the battlefield.

When Confederate General Robert E. Lee surrendered to Union General Ulysses S. Grant at Appomattox Court House, Virginia, on April 9, 1865, the military war effectively ended, but the religious war only moved into an even higher intensity. The Northern clergy eagerly interpreted the Union victory as a sign of God's pleasure with the North. "I charge the whole guilt of this war upon the ambitious, educated, plotting political leaders of the South," thundered the Brooklyn, New York, preacher Henry Ward Beecher, brother to Harriet Beecher Stowe, in 1865. Someday, he continued, "These guiltiest and most remorseless traitors, these high and cultured men with might and wisdom . . . shall be whirled aloft and plunged downward forever and ever in an endless retribution."

The Southern clergy proved themselves equally unrepentant. Although none could deny that the South had been vanquished, few Southern Christians saw the defeat as a sign of divine displeasure. Rather they interpreted their situation as a trial. God chastised the children he truly loved, did he not? Americans had always been prone to say that

God's purposes echoed the nation's. But nowhere did civil religion flourish so grandly as in the Old South during and after the War Between the States. By the 1870s former Confederates talked reverently about the Lost Cause, or the Southern way of life, almost as if it were a religion itself.

But even if most Northern and Southern Christians saw God's blessing upon their respective regions, not all did. One of America's greatest Presidents, who would be assassinated on Good Friday of 1865, rose above regional passions to reflect on the religious meaning of the war.

What was Lincoln's own religion? This question has provoked heated debate. On the one hand, we know that as a young lawyer in Illinois Lincoln rebelled against the rigidity of his parents' Baptist faith and the unseemliness of Christian churches fighting each other as ardently as they had fought the devil. One of Lincoln's political foes in Illinois, the Methodist circuit rider Peter Cartwright, went so far as to say that Lincoln held no religion at all. After the President's death even some of his

This photograph by Mathew Brady captured Catholic services in a Civil War camp. Religious gatherings, which structured both northern and southern army life, brought moments of hope in the midst of death and destruction.

Presbyterian pastor Isaac W. K. Handy (standing, second from left) of Portsmouth, Virginia, found himself imprisoned by Federals in 1861 for 15 months. He used this time to teach theology to his fellow Confederate prisoners.

closest friends said the same. They had a case. Lincoln was the only President who never joined a church, and he never publicly affirmed any of the main doctrines of Christianity.

On the other hand, in his childhood home the inquisitive Abe heard the Bible quoted often. He may have memorized the Psalms and most of the New Testament. As an adult, Lincoln regularly attended a Presbyterian church, both at home in Springfield and in Washington, D.C. He quoted the Bible often, which suggests that he read it regularly. Most importantly, however, his maturity and tragedy prompted Lincoln to think about the larger meaning of life. The legacy of his parents' stern beliefs that all people were predestined by God to go to heaven or to hell, the untimely deaths of two of his four young sons, and the mounting suffering of the war taught Lincoln to see God as a deity who loomed above the wishes of factions and regions no less than those of individuals.

Consider the religious themes in Lincoln's second inaugural address, given less than a month before his death. Each side had looked for an easy triumph, he began, but it was not to be. Both sides read the same Bible and prayed to the same God, invoking his aid against the enemy. Lincoln expressed dismay that anyone would seek God's help in perpetuating slavery, yet he immediately added (following Jesus's words in the New Testament) that no one should judge another's motives. "The prayers of both could not be answered; that of neither has been answered fully."

Then Lincoln rose to one of the most profound religious reflections in American history. God, he judged, had allowed this "terrible war" to come in order to punish both sides for allowing slavery. No one could know how long the Almighty would permit the killing to continue, for "every drop of blood" drawn by the slave master's lash would have to be paid for with the sword. And who could question God's purposes? "[As] was said three thousand years ago, so still it must be said: 'The judgments of the Lord are true and righteous altogether.'"

Did Christianity cause the Civil War? No. But Christians contributed to making a peaceful solution to the scandal of slavery impossible. Did Christians acknowledge their guilt in the matter? Rarely. Still, a few, including the President, sensed the mystery of God's ways with defiant humans. That sense did not atone for all the killing, let alone for slavery, but it may have made Americans more humble about their complicity in the two great tragedies of the age.

QUEEN CITY SIGN CO.
SIGNS AND SHOW CARDS OF EVERY DESCRIPTION
Oil Cloth & Muslin ADVERTISING SIGNS A SPECIALTY.
OLD KENTUCKY WHISKEY
A WIENERWURST WITH EACH DRINK.
EACH DRINK
SIGNS CAREFULLY REMOVED HUNG.
LAGER BEE
THE BEST
K. OF L. CIGARS & TOBACCO.
A WIENERWURST FREE WITH EACH DRINK.
A HOT WEINERW
JOE'S PLACE
DRINK

Chapter 7

Immigrants

Faith of our fathers! living still In spite of dungeon,
fire and sword: O how our hearts beat high with joy,
Whene'er we hear that glorious word:
holy faith! We will be true to thee till death.
  —*Frederick W. Faber, "Faith of Our Fathers" (1849)*

O scar Handlin, a distinguished U.S. historian, once said that he set out to write the story of immigration to America and ended up writing the story of America itself. He spoke well. Statistics never give the whole account of anything, but in this case they provide at least a hint of the vastness of the changes that overtook the nation between 1820 and 1920. In the 1820s, some 140,000 immigrants, almost all European, streamed into the young republic. In the 1830s that number rose to 600,000; in the 1840s, 1.7 million; and in the 1850s, 2.6 million. The 1860s, a decade torn by the Civil War, saw a slight drop, but in the 1870s the rate shot up again, to 2.8 million. Between 1881 and the outbreak of World War I some 35 years later, 23 million more arrived. This seemingly ceaseless river of humanity finally shrank to a trickle only when Congress imposed severe restrictions upon immigration in the early 1920s.

The overwhelming majority of the late-19th-century immigrants were Roman Catholics. Many, probably most, were fairly inactive yet loyal members of the church. The growth of Catholics as a percentage of the larger population is startling. The first U.S. census, taken in 1790, showed

In 1890, more than half of Cincinnati's residents were first- or second-generation German Americans, many living in German neighborhoods such as this one. German traditionalists in America believed in protecting their culture, churches, and schools from the influence of other traditions and beliefs.

that 85 percent of white Americans came from British Protestant traditions. At that time less than 2 percent of the white population claimed to be Catholic. But things changed dramatically over the next 70 years. By the opening of the Civil War in 1861, 10 percent of the population identified itself as Catholic, making it one of the largest religious groups in the United States. (Different accounts rendered different figures, but all placed Roman Catholics among the six largest groups.) The surge of Catholic immigration continued apace after the War Between the States. By 1906 fully 17 percent of the population said they were Catholic.

U.S. history did not, of course, begin in the 19th century, and neither did Catholic history. Spanish Franciscans reached Florida in the 1560s and northern New Mexico in the 1590s. Indeed, the oldest continually used church in the United States, the San Miguel Mission in Santa Fe, New Mexico, dates from 1609, more than a decade before the Pilgrims touched Plymouth Rock. But the Spanish, Mexican, and Indian Catholics of the Southwest did not figure prominently in the development of U.S. religion until after World War II. That honor fell to the English Catholics who settled in Maryland in the 1630s and then, especially, to the successive waves of Catholic immigrants who came from Ireland, Germany, Poland, Italy, and eastern Europe in the latter two-thirds of the 19th century.

John Carroll, the first Catholic bishop in the United States, exemplified the high social status of English Catholics at the beginning of the 19th century. His younger cousin Charles Carroll signed the Declaration of Independence, and his older brother Daniel Carroll won a footnote in the history books as a signer of the Constitution. Carroll himself, born the son of a wealthy Maryland merchant in 1735, was educated by Jesuits in France. He returned to Maryland two years before the Revolution to serve as a parish pastor. Both lay people and the pope soon recognized Carroll's exceptional abilities. He rose through the ranks, becoming Vicar Apostolic (leader) of the Mission in the United States in 1784, bishop five years later, and archbishop in 1808. Carroll's non-Christian friend Ben Franklin once urged the pope to appoint Carroll bishop! Carroll strongly supported the separation of church and state. His many

HELP WANTED
NO IRISH NEED APPLY

accomplishments included founding Georgetown Academy for boys near Washington, D.C., in 1789, which evolved into one of the nation's most distinguished universities.

The ethnic makeup of the Catholic Church in the United States started to change noticeably in the 1820s. The long-range source of that change stemmed from the modernization of farming techniques in Europe, which drove millions of peasants off their land in search of jobs. The immediate source stemmed from farming depressions that struck Ireland in the 1820s, followed by a decade of crop failures in the 1840s. During those desperate years some 1.5 million souls starved to death. Another 2.5 million—20 percent of the total population—emigrated from the Emerald Isle in search of food and work. Nearly 2 million of those came to the United States, almost all of them Catholic.

The successive waves of Irish immigrants quickly overwhelmed and eventually displaced the comfortable reign of the English (and some French) Catholics on U.S. soil. The Irish dominated the church's membership rolls through the middle third of the century and controlled the church's hierarchy until the late 20th century. In the process they set the church's tone for the better part of two centuries.

Rank-and-file Irish Catholics had a distinctive approach to their faith. For one thing, they held the church and the clergy in high esteem. Back in Ireland the church had helped resist the English Protestants who had oppressed them for centuries. Because Irish Catholics had been accustomed to looking to the church for protection against the English, in the United States they looked to the church for protection against unscrupulous bosses. Church officials in turn readily supported political

Fear of Catholics, and Irish Catholics in particular, prompted discrimination. A spirited 19th-century Irish-American song poked fun at the bigots, beginning: I'm a decent Irish lad just landed from the town of Ballyfad; / I want a situation and I want it very bad. / I've seen employment advertised. "It's just the thing," says I, / But the dirty spalpeen [rascal] ended with "No Irish Need Apply."

figures who assisted their people—one thinks especially of the Irish Catholic political dynasties in Boston and New York. Moreover, traditions brought from the homeland encouraged Irish Catholics to raise large families, to insist upon strict sexual morality, and to uphold traditional beliefs in matters of doctrine.

In the middle years of the century the Irish found themselves competing with a new wave of migrants, this time from the German-speaking provinces of central Europe. Some 400,000 Germans arrived in the 1840s, and nearly a million more in the 1850s. Again, many were Catholic—but with a difference. Where the Irish had settled mostly in the towns and cities of the Northeast, the Germans now established themselves mostly in the Upper Midwest, in a triangle defined by Milwaukee, St. Louis, and Cincinnati. Occupational and class differences emerged too. The Irish worked mainly in mines and factories, while Germans labored mostly on farms and in towns as craftsmen and shopkeepers. And where the Irish remained poor, often bordering upon destitution, the Germans were generally self-sufficient and often quite prosperous.

Beyond these social differences, the Irish and the Germans represented quite different ways of relating to the largely Protestant environment. The Irish found it easier to engage outsiders, partly because they spoke English. The German Catholics, on the other hand, resisted assimilation. They felt that they could best preserve their faith by worshiping in German, sending their children to German parochial schools, and associating only with other Germans. At one point the antagonism between Irish and German Catholics grew so intense that Germans in New York City tried to establish their own cemetery so that they could still shun the Irish after death.

After the Civil War new waves of Catholic immigrants from other parts of Europe started to wash across U.S. shores. The most conspicuous of the postwar migrations included Poles and Italians. More than 2 million Polish Catholics arrived between 1850 and 1924. Like the Irish, they proved intensely loyal to their church. Indeed, for many daily life revolved around church activities. At the Sacred Heart parish in New Britain, Connecticut, for example, the church established a school, an orphanage, an

A Nun's Letter to Germany

Nuns shouldered more than their share of the hard, day-to-day work of planting and nurturing the Catholic faith on American shores. Their lack of familiarity with American ways compounded the difficulty of dealing with an overwhelming Protestant majority. In this 1847 letter to Father Mathias Siegert back home in Munich, Germany, Mother Theresa Gerhardinger vented her frustrations.

[In America, schools] will not become large, for there are too many of them, and attendance is voluntary, which is bad. Children attend one school today, another tomorrow, just as they please. If they are corrected they do not come back; learning they often consider recreation. All they want to do is eat cookies, taffy and molasses candy, a cheap sweet. This causes us much trouble. If we forbid it they threaten not to come to school any more. At the slightest punishment the parents say, "In this country one may not treat children so severely; they, too, must be given freedom." They do not listen to any one, and even strike their parents if they do not give in to them. They laugh and jeer at priests. . . . They will not write one letter of the alphabet at home. "I go to school for that," is their answer. Homework cannot be introduced here; the parents do not want it either. . . . They do not manifest the slightest eagerness to learn German. . . . All one hears is English. If they want to insult each other they say, "You German!"

old-age home, a newspaper, and a cemetery, all run by sisters (women religious persons) of the parish. Also like the Germans, the Polish Catholics wanted to worship in their native language and avoid needless association with Protestants. Another trait the Poles shared with the Germans was resentment of the Irish. As far as the Poles could see, the Irish bishops and archbishops ran the Catholic Church in the United States mostly for the benefit of the Irish.

Italian Catholics, who also started arriving in large numbers in the latter half of the century, left their distinctive mark on the religious landscape as well. Until 1870 northern Italy remained divided politically from southern Italy and Sicily. Northern Italian Catholics gained a reputation for learning, artistic achievement, and religious restraint. Southern Italian Catholics, in contrast, gained a reputation for intense piety, marked by fervent emotionalism and (in the view of outsiders) irregular beliefs and practices. The latter included carnival-like street festivals, or *festas,* involving days of celebration and parading in honor of the patron saints of local towns or regions.

Another big difference separated the two regions and two forms of Catholicism. The North of Italy enjoyed good relations with the papacy, the South did not. Hence, when southern Italian Catholics came to the United States they resisted the church and the clergy, preferring to carry out their devotional practices in the home, if at all. And they too resented the Irish, who dominated the church and seemed determined to keep the best appointments for themselves.

By now it should be evident that the Catholic Church in America in the 19th century faced enormous challenges. It had to cope with internal diversity almost as bewildering as the diversity of the Protestant denominations. But the church enjoyed one advantage the Protestants did not. It was the oldest continuous institution in the Western world. The sense of tradition and the ever-present resource (or threat) of theological direction from Rome enabled the church to stand as a rock of stability in a rapidly changing environment.

Putting aside their ethnic differences, bishops, priests, and nuns rolled up their sleeves and went to work. They built churches, of course, but also

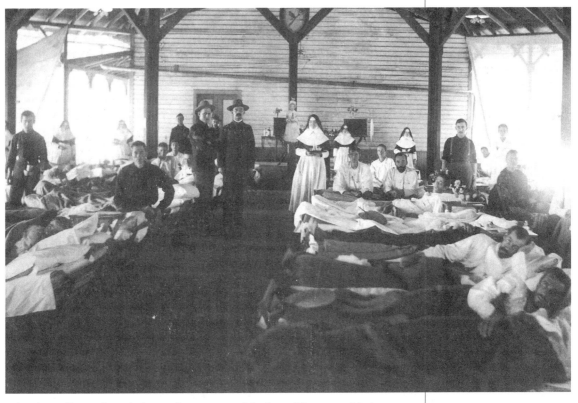

The Sisters of Mercy presided over many hospital wards during the Spanish-American War of 1898. This photograph shows a ward in a pavilion in Turner Park, in Knoxville, Tennessee, that was converted for the purpose.

schools, colleges, hospitals, orphanages, and lodges. They provided emergency funds for the destitute and medical treatment for the sick. They helped frightened immigrants who knew no English to find housing and jobs. They shielded laborers from shifty bosses. They served as intermediaries between the immigrants and city officials. They established the largest private school system in the world, mostly staffed by nuns. Scores of nuns served heroically as nurses and cooks in the Civil War and the Spanish-American War of 1898. One prominent order, the Sisters of Mercy, established and ran one of the larger hospital systems in the United States.

Catholic clergy and sisters distinguished themselves for their ability simultaneously to tend both the physical and the spiritual needs of immigrants. Elizabeth Bayley Seton, for example, won distinction doing both. Reared as an Episcopalian in New York City after the Revolution, Seton and her husband journeyed to Italy in 1803 in the hope that the warm Mediterranean sun might reverse his deteriorating health. He met an

Elizabeth Ann Seton converted to Catholicism after attending Catholic churches during her travels in Italy. Shortly afterward, she founded the Sisters of Charity, who knew her as Mother Seton.

untimely death, but Seton found comfort in the concern and piety of the local Catholics who cared for her. She also found her life's calling.

Returning to the United States, Seton converted to the Catholic Church. She soon moved to Baltimore to escape the harsh criticism of relatives and friends who were appalled that a Protestant would stoop to become a Catholic. In Baltimore, Seton established the Sisters of Charity in 1809. She soon moved to a beautiful valley near Emmitsburg, Maryland, where the Sisters opened St. Joseph's Academy as well as a free school. They nursed the sick and needy in that area. The Sisters then fanned out to other cities in the East and on to the West. In St. Louis they built the first hospital west of the Mississippi River. Seton died in her 46th year, but in 1975 the church canonized her, making her the first American saint.

As the nation sprawled westward across the Appalachians and into the desert Southwest and California, the church followed. Bishop Jean-Baptiste Lamy, the mid-century cleric immortalized in Willa Cather's 1927 novel *Death Comes for the Archbishop*, typified the bravery of the Catholic clergy:

> During the first year after his arrival in Santa Fe, the Bishop was actually in his diocese only about four months. Six months of that first year were consumed in attending the Plenary Council at Baltimore. . . . He went on horseback over the Santa Fe trail to St. Louis, nearly a thousand miles, then by steamboat to Pittsburgh, across the mountains to Cumberland, and on to Washington by the new railroad. The return journey was even slower, as he had with him the five nuns who came to found the school of Our Lady of Light.

Dispatched from France (where he was born) to serve as a missionary in Ohio, Lamy had been appointed Vicar Apostolic of New Mexico in 1850. Traveling mostly on horseback, fighting thirst, heat, and sun, Lamy brought the vast, largely uncharted territories of Arizona, New Mexico, and much of Colorado under his jurisdiction. With the aid of many now-nameless sisters, Lamy attended to the spiritual needs of the 100,000 Catholic Indians living in those regions.

Success proved to be costly, however, for the church's growing visibility invited growing persecution. In the United States Catholics had rarely enjoyed the same liberties as Protestants. In colonial times even Pennsylvania, which prided itself on its high degree of religious toleration, restricted Catholics from voting, holding public office, or celebrating mass in public. But on the whole Catholics managed reasonably well in early English-speaking America, especially after the Revolutionary War, when they basked in Catholic France's support of the patriot cause. But things changed dramatically, and for the worse, in the 1830s.

Many factors accounted for Protestants' fears of the Catholics. Most fundamentally, the Catholic religion was different. Though Catholics and Protestants shared many assumptions, important distinctions separated them. Most Protestants believed in the right of congregations to choose their own pastors, in the final authority of the Bible, and in salvation through faith in Jesus Christ. Most Catholics, on the other hand, believed that churches should be run by bishops and priests, that final authority should rest in the church's interpretation of the Bible, and that material sacraments like bread and wine, assisted by saints, mediated salvation. Many Protestants felt that Catholics were mired in the mud of superstition. President Thomas Jefferson, for example, despised the Roman Catholic Church for resisting modern science and rationality.

Other suspicions aggravated religious differences. For the better part of 400 years Protestants had believed that the pope in Rome embodied the Antichrist (the evil world ruler described in the New Testament Book of Revelation). Prejudices so deeply rooted were not easy to shake, even in the sunlit optimism of the New World. Class and cultural antagonisms further darkened the picture. The Irish, desperate for work, were willing to toil at rock-bottom pay, thus undercutting the wages of the laborers already present. (In time the Irish and German Catholics would despise Polish, Italian, and other newcomers for precisely the same reason.) And Catholics often displayed cultural habits that seemed alien if not downright dangerous to the Protestant majority. They gambled. They played sports on Sunday. And just when the Protestants felt that they were beginning to win the battle against alcohol, the Catholics arrived with strong attachments to their pubs and beer gardens. Beyond that, Catholics got their news from foreign-language newspapers, sent their children to their own schools, and even buried their dead in their own cemeteries. Protestants wondered, why so much secrecy?

And then there was the problem of democracy. Protestants believed that the long history of the Catholic Church in Europe proved that the church would tyrannize the state if it got the chance (Archbishop Carroll's efforts to assert Catholic patriotism notwithstanding). These Protestant suspicions were indeed grounded upon some fact. For centuries the papacy had insisted that the church ultimately should control the state. When democratic revolutions swept Europe in the late 1840s, the pope condemned them. In 1864 the pope issued a letter (called an encyclical) attacking modern errors, including the notion of church-state separation. And then there was slavery, which the church had failed to condemn, for complex theological reasons. Moreover, rank-and-file Irish laborers in the North, who rioted in New York City in 1863, feared that free blacks would rob them of jobs. Whatever the explanation, the church appeared to favor Old World traditions of repression and privilege.

One more factor loomed large in Protestants' suspicions. They suspected that Catholics might succeed all too well in the free air of the New World, even winning converts from Protestant churches. There is no evidence that large numbers of Protestants actually converted, but a number of prominent intellectuals did. Isaac Hecker showed what could happen. Born to a prosperous German family in New York in 1819, Hecker first attended a Methodist church, then joined a Transcendentalist community near Boston. (Among other things, Transcendentalists believed in radical economic and social equality.) But Hecker found himself drawn to the lush rituals of the Catholic Church. More importantly, he grew persuaded that the Christian tree, with its hundreds of branches, all stemmed from a single trunk: the Roman Catholic Church.

Thus, at the age of 25 Hecker converted. Fourteen years later he founded one of the most famous of Catholic orders for men, the Paulist

Fathers. Hecker spent the rest of his busy life seeking to bring lax Catholics back to the faith through vibrant preaching and impassioned writing. He targeted Protestants, trying to persuade them that the Catholic Church not only offered the truth, but also that it offered hope and strength for America. A democratic land needed the unity and stability of an ancient faith.

The Protestants reacted, sometimes vigorously, sometimes viciously, and even at times violently. Lyman Beecher, then president of Lane Theological Seminary in Ohio, unleashed his fears in an 1832 book called *A Plea for the West.* In this influential volume Beecher warned that America would lose its democratic freedoms if the Protestant majority allowed Catholics to overrun the newly opening territories of the West. After all, he grumbled, Catholics were accustomed to slavish obedience to the pope.

Other Protestants established newspapers to combat the perceived Catholic peril. One carried the revealing title *Protestant Vindicator.* Others turned out propaganda tracts about cruelty, enslavement of women, sexual immorality, and even infant murder in convents. Two of the most notorious were called "Six Months in a Convent" (1835) and "Awful Disclosures of the Hotel Dieu Nunnery of Montreal" (1836). The 1850s saw the brief rise of a new political party devoted to curbing the imagined Catholic threat. The Know-Nothings, as they were popularly called, nominated former President Millard Fillmore as a Presidential candidate in 1852 and actually sent 75 men to Congress two years later.

After the Civil War, relations between Protestants and Catholics slowly improved. Several factors helped. For one thing, thousands of Irish served in the Union army with valor. Also, many Catholics, especially Germans, had risen in economic, social, and educational status and thus posed less of a threat to Protestant workers. By the final third of the century many

Father Isaac Hecker, who founded the Paulist Fathers, strove to bring Protestants back to Catholicism, which he considered to be the primary Christian faith. Here he wears the long cassock of the Paulist fathers and the Mission Cross.

Catholic leaders, particularly Irish ones, began to think that they had more to gain than to lose by cooperating with the Protestant majority.

Those who advocated cooperation came to be known as Americanists. Irish bishops and priests dominated the Americanist faction in the Catholic Church (although a few, such as Hecker, were German). The Americanists loved their church and, precisely for that reason, felt that Catholics should embrace America. In their view Catholics needed to play a more prominent role in public affairs. With that end in mind, the first U.S. cardinal, James Gibbons of Baltimore, went so far as to speak at the World's Parliament of Religions in Chicago in 1893. Gibbons did not think Catholic Christianity could be reduced to other forms of Christianity, let alone other religions, but he thought that talking with religious outsiders was better than ignoring or scorning them.

John Ireland, the archbishop of St. Paul, Minnesota, also effectively represented the Americanists' outlook. "We should live in our age, know it, be in touch with it," Ireland insisted in 1889. "Let no one dare to paint her brow with a foreign taint or pin to her mantle foreign linings." Ireland put teeth into his admonition. He doubted that Catholics should isolate their children by sending them to parochial schools. To be sure, this was a tough question. Most public schools taught history through a Protestant lens, extolled Protestant heroes, and read from the thoroughly Protestant King James Authorized Version of the Bible. Yet Ireland felt that Catholic children could thrive in a pluralistic environment.

Others were not so sure. The traditionalists, typically German, coveted the value of preaching in their own language and maintaining the rich musical and liturgical heritage of German Catholic worship. The traditionalists urged Catholics to reap the economic and political benefits of living in the United States, but harbored dark suspicions about whether any good could come from needless interaction in matters of culture. In some ways the traditionalists seemed out of step with the times, but they understood, more clearly than the Americanists, how easily love for the land could displace love of the church.

In the end, Pope Leo XIII largely agreed with the traditionalists. Official letters he issued in 1895 and 1899 urged U.S. Catholics to remember

that separation of church and state was not the ideal. Loyal Catholics should not be swept away, he wrote, by the popular but erroneous idea that democracy was king—an idea he indirectly, and somewhat unfairly, attributed to the Catholic Americanists. Christ was king, and the church, though flawed, represented Christ's will on earth.

At the end of the century Catholics could take pride in vast achievements. They had become the largest Christian denomination in the United States. They had established an impressive system of schools, hospitals, and mutual benefit societies. They had helped millions of immigrants adjust to American life. And they had kept the faith. They emerged from the intellectual storms of the late 19th century with their theological foundations still firmly intact (some said too much so). By any reasonable measure of such things the church had reached maturity. Just after the turn of the century, in 1908, the pope acknowledged that fact by officially declaring the church no longer a mission (a dependent outpost). Henceforth it would stand on its own as the Roman Catholic Church in the United States of America.

Although Roman Catholics remained much larger in numbers and cultural influence, Orthodox Catholics maintained their own quiet presence in American life. The latter resembled Roman Catholics in several respects. They both worshiped with rich liturgies, decorated their churches elaborately, and preserved a strong sense of tradition. Orthodox

This 1870 cartoon blames bitterness between the races and religions on the practice of having separate schools for different religious and ethnic groups. The solution, it suggests, is for all children to attend non-sectarian public schools.

Catholics resembled Protestants, however, in that they placed final authority in the ancient creeds of Christianity, not the pope in Rome. And more than either Roman Catholics or Protestants, the Orthodox pursued a mystical union with God as the highest aim of the religious life. Architectural splendor aided that aim. Their churches, often exceptionally beautiful, were (and remain) recognizable by an onion-shaped dome or domes at the top, often brightly painted.

The Orthodox originated in the countries hugging the eastern rim of the Mediterranean, primarily Greece, Albania, and Syria, as well as Russia. In the middle of the 18th century Russian traders, explorers, and fur trappers started streaming into the vast wilderness of Alaska. Monks followed in the 1790s. The Orthodox stamped their faith upon the landscape, giving their outposts luminous names like Three Saints Harbor and New Archangel. When the United States bought Alaska from Russia

As American Catholics debated whether the church should conform to American ways and democracy or should carefully guard its traditions and its connection to Rome, Pope Leo XIII (seated in his carriage) supported the traditionalist viewpoint.

This Russian Orthodox cathedral in Sitka, Alaska, is topped by a slender onion dome. Russian Orthodox monks began crossing the Bering Strait into Alaska more than a century before this picture was taken in 1900.

in 1867, the Orthodox were already well rooted there. So well rooted, in fact, that they soon spread down the Pacific Coast into northern California. This made the Russian Orthodox Church the only major religious group (until the late 20th century) that had moved from the west to the east. At the end of the 19th century the Orthodox reported only 90,000 members, but in the next hundred years that figure would swell to 3.5 million. Many said that Orthodox believers constituted the fourth major religious tradition in America, alongside the Catholics, Protestants, and Jews. However defined, they added another richly colored tile to the American religious mosaic.

Chapter 8

Innovators

Thou art giving and forgiving, ever blessing, ever blest,
wellspring of the joy of living, ocean depth of happy rest!
Thou our Father, Christ our Brother-all who live in love are thine;
Teach us how to love each other, lift us to the joy divine.
—*Henry Van Dyke, "Joyful, Joyful, We Adore Thee" (1907)*

ust after the turn of the 20th century Henry Adams sat down to write his autobiography, *The Education of Henry Adams*. Looking back over a distinguished career as a teacher at Harvard, he wondered whether the outlook of a child born in 1854 was closer to 1904 or to the beginning of Christianity. Adams had good reason to wonder. In the 50 years from the Civil War to World War I, thoughtful men and women everywhere formed powerful new ideas about the immanent (intimately close) nature of God, the human authorship of the Bible, the evolutionary origin of human beings, and the similarities between the Hebrew-Christian tradition and other major religions of the world. New notions won acceptance because they seemed more credible in the modern world. The people who refined and spread these new ideas gave themselves various labels but, for the sake of simplicity, we shall call them all innovators.

If we think of innovators as people who were prepared to challenge old ideas in the light of science and the expanding horizons of world discovery, then innovators had been around for a long time. Decades before the Revolutionary War, for example, many Puritans had doubted their

Representatives of religions around the world traveled to Chicago in 1893 for the World Parliament of Religions, held in conjunction with the World's Columbian Exposition. Many participants came from Japan, China, and India, in particular.

parents' view of God as a stern, judgmental deity. They insisted instead that God was both too rational and too kind-hearted to cast anyone into hell. During the Revolutionary era a small but influential group of men and women, including founders such as Benjamin Franklin and Thomas Jefferson, came to more startling conclusions. They believed that God had created the world as a finely tuned machine, much like a jeweler fashioning an exquisite clock. Once the world was made, God would not disturb it with miracles any more than a jeweler would disturb a perfectly running clock. By the same token, stories in the Bible that seemed inconsistent with God's rational, moral nature had to go. One example was the Genesis legend about Abraham and Isaac. In that ancient account, the Lord instructed Abraham to take his son Isaac to a distant mountaintop, build an altar, lay Isaac upon the altar, then slay him and burn his body as a holy sacrifice. Abraham dutifully obeyed each step, until the Lord sent an angel to stay his hand just before he was to plunge the knife. Stories of that sort now seemed immoral.

In the mid-19th century innovators found an eloquent new voice in the ideas of Ralph Waldo Emerson. Born into an elite Unitarian family in Boston in 1803, Emerson served as a Unitarian pastor in that city until he concluded that he no longer believed even the stripped-down claims of that tradition. Emerson spent the rest of his life in the nearby town of Concord, writing essays and lecturing to almost anyone who would listen. He challenged traditionalists to test religious concepts for themselves. Everyone, Emerson insisted, must make their own decisions about what was true about God, humans, and the world. In the grand tradition of American individualism Emerson concluded that the only valid authority was the authority of each person's private judgment.

Emerson plunged ahead, boldly, without fear of others' views. The Concord sage argued that God was not a stern judge, not a kind grandfather, and not a distant clock-maker. Instead, God was best understood as a spirit, an ideal, a breath of life, everywhere and always filling the world with the inexhaustible power of the divine presence. God, he said, was as close as the atmosphere, as intimate as the "blowing clover and the falling rain." And if God was everywhere, then miracles were not necessary.

This painting of *Abraham's Sacrifice* from the Old Testament captures the moment when an angel stops Abraham from killing his son, Isaac, as an offering to God. God only wanted to test Abraham's faith, and the angel shows Abraham a ram to sacrifice instead of his son. Many believers did not know how to interpret such Bible stories because they seemed to imply that God was irrational.

Indeed, they were not even possible, because God could hardly impose a miracle—a violation of natural law—upon himself.

That insight led Emerson to ask a bigger question: If God really was everywhere, how did people know about him? By reading the Bible? By listening to the pronouncements of the bishops of the church? No. People knew God through intuition, especially when they applied their intuitive

Transcendentalist writer Ralph Waldo Emerson perceived that God was everywhere, and that all people had to do to experience God was commune with the world around them, especially nature.

abilities to the wonders of nature. People sensed God's reality in the same way they sensed the reality of other human beings. God remained beneath the surface appearances of the natural world, just as a friend's personality remained beneath the surface appearances of his or her physical body. Because truth transcended the ordinary realm of daily sense perception, Emerson and an elite band of like-minded friends called themselves Transcendentalists.

Emerson's pioneering concepts opened the floodgates to other ideas. In the 1870s, 1880s, and 1890s a torrent of new religious notions surged across the landscape. Taken together they changed the way in which millions of people in all stations of life thought about things heavenly and earthly.

Fresh thoughts about the nature of the Bible came first. Close attention to the content of the Bible was nothing new. For many centuries preachers and rabbis had carefully studied the text of the scriptures in order to know exactly what they said and meant as a guide for life. But the late 19th century witnessed special attention to questions of authorship. Who wrote the different parts of the Bible? How did those authors reflect the assumptions and prejudices of their times? How did the Bible acquire its present list of books of vastly differing length and literary style? The men and women who pressed such questions came to be known as higher critics (versus the so-called lower critics, who busied themselves primarily with the "lower" or less controversial task of finding accurate texts and creating precise translations). The answers the higher critics came up with proved exciting to some, profoundly disturbing to others.

Charles Augustus Briggs was one of those who wrestled with these matters. A Presbyterian Old Testament professor at Union Theological

Seminary in New York City at the end of the century, Briggs gained a reputation for brilliant, outspoken advocacy. By the end of his career, tens of thousands had heard of him. Some responded with approval, many others with sharp disapproval, leading to his removal from the church for heresy in 1893. Briggs insisted that the Bible should be read as any other ancient text, without imposing supernatural explanations. For example, the Bible claimed that a great fish swallowed the prophet Jonah and then regurgitated him unharmed three days later. Should claims of that sort be accepted as factually true, no matter how much they strained credibility? Or should they be assessed as other ancient legends would be, as prescientific myths, or perhaps as poetry, carrying a moral meaning? To be sure, Briggs, like many innovators, was not entirely consistent. He felt that some miracles, such as the virgin birth of Christ, rested upon solid evidence, especially if one looked to the data contained in the ancient creeds. But on the whole he urged Christians and Jews to be more critical about what was demonstrably true and what was mere legend in the Bible.

The rise of modern science in general, and the evolutionary view of human origins in particular, posed a second major challenge to traditional ideas. At first glance there was nothing new about evolutionary theories. Believers on both sides of the Atlantic had long accepted the great antiquity of the earth. Many had early on doubted the literal truth of the Adam and Eve story. Many had recognized that animals had evolved within species, so that larger dogs had emerged from smaller dogs, or darker horses from lighter ones. Many too had acknowledged the terrible cruelty of nature, for creatures often survived by killing and eating others.

But these ideas became more startling with the publication in England in 1859 of Charles Darwin's massive book *The Origin of Species by Means of Natural Selection.* In it this English scientist introduced Americans to the disturbing notion of natural selection. According to this principle, all plants and animals, including humans, changed over time in response to changes in the natural environment. Thus, if the climate in a particular region grew colder, animals that happened to be born there with thicker and warmer coats were more likely to survive than those

This engraving illustrates Charles Darwin's discovery that finches in different habitats in the Galapagos Islands developed distinctive beaks that best allowed them to gather food, such as a thick beak for cracking nuts and seeds (far left) or a thin, curved beak for drilling insects out of cacti (far right). Darwin's theory of natural selection distressed many people because it seemed to contradict their religious beliefs.

with lighter coats. The obvious similarities between humans and primates, or the equally obvious fact that nature was a battleground drenched in red, could now be satisfactorily explained. Many intellectuals found Darwin's theories liberating, for they enabled thoughtful men and women in all parts of the United States to make sense of the natural world. Lyman Abbott, editor of the influential religious periodical *The Outlook,* jauntily embraced evolution as "God's way of doing things."

Darwin did not intend to upset anyone's faith, but he did, perhaps more than any other thinker of the 19th century. The idea, inferred from Darwin's book, that all natural processes proceeded at random, like the roll of dice, upset many believers. But that was not the worst of it. If the principle of natural selection were true, then the only measure of good or bad actions was survival. The Hebrew prophets' and Christ's teachings about personal sacrifice in the interest of a higher cause seemed pointless. To suggest that the Adam and Eve story was mere legend seemed bad enough, but to argue that Jewish and Christian moral teachings equaled only warm sentiments—sentiments that could be discarded whenever they appeared to block progress—seemed immeasurably worse.

A growing awareness of religions in other parts of the world formed a third major challenge to older ideas. For thousands of years Jews and Christians had firmly believed that the biblical tradition remained different from all other faiths. Jews thought that God had called them alone to be the bearers of God's law. Christians believed that God had singled them out to be the bearers of the message of salvation. American Jews and Christians had long known, of course, that many other religions existed. As far back as 1784 Hannah Adams, possibly the first woman in America to make her living by writing, had published a *Dictionary of All Religions.* But until the late 19th century that knowledge remained mostly theoretical, mediated through rare travelers' reports and romantic tales about faraway places.

This narrow outlook changed dramatically in the 1880s and especially in the 1890s. In those decades the rest of the world arrived at America's doorstep and knocked—insistently. Many factors were involved. The rapid development of shipping and railroad technology helped the expansion of trade. Military muscle flexing took thousands of young men to distant lands. So did increasing wealth, which allowed vacation travel to places other than Europe for the upper-middle and upper classes.

The Foreign Missionary newsletter encouraged Presbyterians to devote themselves to missionary work in foreign lands, such as Canton, China, in the bottom picture.

Above all, the rapid growth of Christian missions themselves fostered a new and worrisome fear that the Hebrew-Christian tradition was not unique. Young men and women from small towns in New England and the Midwest, who had never seen a real Hindu or Muslim, now found themselves face to face with living representatives of those faiths. Hundreds of missionaries, and thousands of their supporters back home, began to suspect that Islam, Hinduism, and especially Buddhism carried highly developed ethical systems of their own. From there it was only a short step to the conclusion that those religions offered equally valid paths to God.

The World's Parliament of Religions, held in conjunction with the Columbian Exposition in Chicago in the fall of 1893, marked a turning point. The parliament may not have been, as one reporter put it, the most important event of the century, but at the time it must have seemed so. For 17 days running, thousands of spectators jammed the Hall of Columbus hoping to catch a glimpse of the colorfully garbed holy men who had traveled from all parts of the earth to describe the faiths of their homelands. For most of those visitors in Chicago, as well as countless men and women who read about the fanfare in hometown newspapers, the parliament offered their first real exposure to any religion besides Judaism or Christianity. Many came away wondering what some missionaries out in the field had suspected for a long time: did not other religions offer their own perfectly respectable paths to God?

In the late 19th century, then, religious innovators both received and contributed to new notions about the Bible, human nature, and the origins of Judaism and Christianity. But innovators did not all think alike. They fell along a spectrum, ranging from agnostics on the left to liberals on the right, with free religionists of various stripes scattered in between. We shall briefly look at each position through the eyes of one representative figure, concentrating on the Protestants, who formed the great majority.

Agnostics, who took their name from a Greek word meaning "no knowledge," believed that humans simply could not know whether a personal God existed or not. Although agnostics never represented more than a tiny minority of Americans in the 19th century, they seemed conspicuous because a disproportionate number of vocal and articulate spokespersons championed this point of view. Robert G. Ingersoll, for example, won enduring fame—and lasting contempt—as a skilled advocate of agnosticism on the lecture circuit. This Congregational pastor's son turned against Christianity when he reached adulthood in the 1850s. Ingersoll held that humans simply had no way of knowing whether God existed or what happened after death. Since one could never know the answer to big questions of this sort, it remained better not to guess, let alone to impose one's beliefs upon others. Ingersoll also scorned efforts to harmonize science and Christianity. In place of idle speculation, he called for a faith that concentrated on improving the human lot in the present world. Use science, he urged, to create a civilization that was more just, more humane, more democratic. Ingersoll's high personal moral standards disarmed critics who feared that his agnosticism would leave society in shambles.

Free religionists occupied something of a middle position on the spectrum. Only a few actually used the term free religionist, but the label fit thousands of maverick spirits who sought to develop their ideas on their own, without the constraint of inherited creeds or communities of faith. Elizabeth Cady Stanton exemplified this outlook. We met her in an earlier chapter as an advocate of woman suffrage and employment rights, but she displayed additional interests too. Born in 1815, Stanton grew up in a sternly Presbyterian home in Johnstown, New York. As a child, however, she recoiled from the "church, the parsonage, the graveyard, and the solemn, tolling bell." She associated institutional Christianity with gloomy teachings about hell, an obsession with saving souls for the afterlife, and a determination to keep people from thinking for themselves. In time she embraced a more nourishing faith. Although this happily married mother of seven argued for a benevolent God, an orderly universe, and the immortality of the individual soul, she doubted that God would interfere in history or give special revelation to particular persons or groups. Late in life Stanton helped write a commentary on the Bible, published in 1895 as *The Woman's Bible,* which sought to expose the repressiveness of the Bible's teachings about women. This tough-minded reformer sought a religion worthy of a free mind.

And then there were the large number of liberals, men and women who positioned themselves closest to traditional ideas. Liberals assumed that faith began in direct experiences of the beauty of God's presence in daily life. Henry Ward Beecher, pastor of Plymouth Congregational Church in Brooklyn, New York, from 1847 until his death in 1887, represented this vein of thought. Beecher was almost as famous as his sister, Harriet Beecher Stowe (author of *Uncle Tom's Cabin).* In an age graced by distinguished preachers—often called princes of the pulpit—Beecher reigned as king. His sermons combined wit, learning, and soaring oratory. People loved him. Most never seemed to notice that his views of Christ, miracles, and future punishment remained hopelessly fuzzy.

Henry Ward Beecher taught a generation of liberal leaders that it was more important to sense God's presence in their hearts than to dream up abstract theories about God in their minds. In this view Jesus was best seen not as the unique Son of God but as an ethical example and a guide for navigating through life's troubled times. The Bible was best read, they argued, as the story of God's saving activities in history.

Liberals like Beecher enjoyed wide influence. They soon dominated the most prestigious divinity schools, including Harvard, Yale, and Chicago. Directly or indirectly they shaped the thinking of thousands of pastors and tens of thousands of Sunday school teachers. By the early 20th century liberals' ideas could be heard from possibly half the Protestant pulpits in the land. Most mainline denominations, especially Baptists, Congregationalists, Disciples, Episcopalians, and Presbyterians in the North and West, were defined by liberals. Their concepts found echoes in other religious traditions too. Reform Jews, in particular, embraced the notions of divine nearness and the importance of social justice. Irish Catholic intellectuals distinguished themselves by their growing appreciation for the insights of modern biblical criticism and the intellectual freedom of America.

Thus, the Old Testament, "in the beginning," proclaims the simultaneous creation of man and woman, the eternity and equality of sex; and the New Testament echoes back through the centuries the individual sovereignty of woman growing out of this natural fact. Paul, in speaking of equality as the very soul and essence of Christianity, said, "There is neither Jew nor Greek, there is neither bond nor free, there is neither male nor female; for ye are all one in Christ Jesus." With this recognition of the feminine element in the Godhead in the Old Testament, and this declaration of the equality of the sexes in the New, we may well wonder at the contemptible status woman occupies in the Christian Church of to-day.

In this handwritten draft of Elizabeth Cady Stanton's 1895 *Women's Bible*, she urges equality of the sexes. Even though God created Adam first, she writes, that does not mean men are superior to women.

Of the three forms of innovative thinkers considered—agnostics, free religionists, and liberals—the last proved by far the most effective in spreading their ideas among millions of ordinary believers. Why did liberals' notions catch on so easily?

First, it helps to remember that liberals' ideas were part of a larger process of rapid change. Urbanization forced people of varying outlooks

Liberal clergymen such as Henry Ward Beecher, pictured with his sister, Harriet Beecher Stowe, presented religion in a way that seemed more in tune with modern ideas.

to live close to each other. Thoughtful persons could no longer assume that their own view of the world was the only one that existed. Moreover, for thousands of years people had lived close to the land, but now indoor labor and human-made time permitted people to suppose that their destiny lay within their control. The rise of research universities such as Cornell, Stanford, Chicago, and Johns Hopkins, and the emergence of scientists as the new elite, played an important role too. University-based researchers increasingly displaced the clergy as the final judges of what was true or not true.

Second, virtually all religious liberals saw themselves not as debunkers but as lonely prophets, helping humankind achieve intellectual freedom. They saw themselves saving, not harming, the core of traditional faith. In their minds the growth of critical methods in the study of history, science, and other cultures had rendered the older notions obsolete. The choice, then, was either to discard faith entirely or rethink and reclaim what was true in light of recent advances in knowledge. They took special pride in their ability to accommodate the old to the new and thus retain the best of both.

Finally, many liberals tried to apply the new ideas to the righting of social wrongs, which brought them in tune with the broader reform impulses of the age. They believed that the most ethically advanced portions of the Bible, as well as the best of modern thought, proved that God was not wrathful but essentially kind hearted. They also believed that the Bible demanded social justice. The older focus upon individual salvation was plainly inadequate. The Hebrew-Christian tradition required all decent, God-fearing men and women to address the terrible disparities of wealth and the inhumane working conditions that crippled American life. In a word, the Bible demanded social justice.

The intellectual challenges of the late 19th century forever changed the landscape of religion in America. The new ideas shaped the thinking of ordinary men and women as profoundly as Copernicus's discovery in the 15th century that the earth moved around the sun. To be sure, many thoughtful men and women resisted the most advanced trends of the age, but none could ignore them. A few of the innovators, like Ingersoll, gave up belief altogether. Others, like Stanton, focused on purging the Hebrew-Christian tradition of its morally and intellectually distasteful features. But most followed Beecher's constructive pattern of seeking creative ways to retain the essence of their faith while taking modern challenges seriously. If in their hands God became less a supernatural being and more an immanent divine presence, he also became a source of enduring comfort in times of breathtaking change.

Chapter 9

Conservatives

O God, our help in ages past,
our hope for years to come,
be Thou our guide while life shall last,
and our eternal home.
  —*Isaac Watts, "O God, Our Help in Ages Past" (1719)*

n the later decades of the 19th century millions of thoughtful Americans acquired a renewed appreciation for the religious wisdom of the past. We call these Americans conservatives because they felt that time-honored truths, tested and refined in the long experience of the human race, offered the most effective way to deal with the intellectual, social, and technological challenges of the modern world.

Religious conservatives came in a bewildering variety of species. Some proved primarily interested in defending the authority and accuracy of the Bible. Others concerned themselves above all with strict standards of personal conduct. Some found their greatest joy in the biblical promise that Jesus Christ would soon return. Still others looked to the traditions of their own extended family or ethnic group for guidance. What they all held in common was a simple though powerful conviction that the past held the key to the future.

From the early 17th century through the late 20th century the Bible formed the bedrock of religious tradition in America. Before the Revolution the Crown barred colonial printers from producing the King James

Cheyenne and Arapaho Indians perform the Ghost Dance in 1898. The Ghost Dance was supposed to speed the departure of whites from the land and reunite the Indians with their dead ancestors. Ironically, white spectators and the American flag preside over this performance.

139

On March 13, 1897, the 25th President, William McKinley, placed his hand on the Bible—as all Presidents have done before and since—as Chief Justice Melville W. Fuller administered the oath of office.

Authorized Version (hoping to protect sales for the king's printers). But after independence Americans rushed to meet the demand for English-language Bibles. Voluntary groups joined them. The largest, the American Bible Society, founded in 1816, was soon producing 300,000 copies per year—for a population under 13 million. (In time the society would print nearly 4 billion Bibles or portions thereof.) Nineteenth-century travelers, encountering town after town bearing names like Eden, Salem, and Bethlehem (not to mention Zoar, Ohio, and Mount Tirzah, North Carolina) might well have imagined themselves wandering through biblical lands in biblical times.

In many families children received intentionally biblical names such as Ezra, Elijah, and Naomi almost as frequently as John, Paul, and Mary (also biblical). All U.S. Presidents took office by swearing an oath on an open Bible. Many Presidents, including Abraham Lincoln, Woodrow Wilson, and Jimmy Carter, memorized large portions of the Scripture and quoted it often. Even Thomas Jefferson, a skeptic, took the trouble to translate and print his own version of the New Testament. The great biblical images of Moses freeing his people, or of the City on a Hill, or of the New Heavens and the New Earth, stirred deep feelings and provided an orientation for life. Jews cherished their Hebrew Scriptures with equal fervor. Some of the bitterest battles fought in the U.S. court system revolved around the proper use of the Bible in public schools—showing, among other things, that the Bible was never inconsequential.

When the literal truthfulness of the Bible came under heavy fire from liberals in the late 19th century, believers everywhere rose to its defense.

Charles Hodge, a theology professor at Princeton Theological Seminary for much of the 19th century, led the charge. Like many Bible scholars, Hodge had studied in Germany, where higher critical approaches to scripture flourished in the universities. He determined to sink the new and, in his mind, destructive ideas before they reached U.S. shores. He believed that the Bible could be proved wholly accurate if its readers would 1) disregard trivial discrepancies in numbers and dates, 2) allow for minor errors of translation and copying over the centuries, 3) distinguish between what the Bible writers personally believed and what they formally taught, and 4) use reasonable or common-sense standards of what constituted accuracy. Thus, if the Bible spoke of the sun rising and setting, that statement should be read as "the language of common life," not as a scientific statement to be taken strictly literally. Hodge boasted that no new idea had ever penetrated Princeton Seminary. What he meant, of course, was that all significant truth had been revealed by God long ago in the Bible. Humans should try to see the full range of meanings the Holy Book contained, not add to or subtract from them.

At the turn of the century the battle between the Bible's critics and its defenders grew more heated, and both sides made extreme statements. After World War I the former came to be known as modernists because they wanted to apply modern standards of scientific credibility to the Bible. The latter, on the other hand, came to be known as fundamentalists because they insisted that the Bible's accuracy in matters of history and science was fundamental (or essential) to the truth of Christianity. The most strident voices won wide publicity, but a majority of Protestants undoubtedly remained closer to the moderately conservative position held by Hodge.

This 1872 cartoon addresses issues of the separation of church and state. Here, a politician (right) is shown offering a deal to an Irishman (left), represented as an immigrant policeman, who wants public schools not only to be Christian, but to be specifically Catholic.

Jesus loves me! This I know, for the Bible tells me so. Little ones to him belong, they are weak, but he is strong. Yes, Jesus loves me! Yes, Jesus loves me! Yes, Jesus loves me! The Bible tells me so.

These words, penned by Anna B. Warner in 1860, not only represented one of the best-loved hymns in American Christianity, but also expressed the piety of millions of ordinary Christians, as traditional as it was heartfelt. Such people worried little about scholars' proofs for the historical accuracy of the Bible. They simply assumed that it could be trusted, especially in matters of faith and morals. This meant seeking forgiveness for their sins and living purified lives—what thousands of Sunday school teachers across the land called conversion and sanctification.

Dwight L. Moody represented this concern. By the time of his death in 1899, this 300-pound evangelist had become the most famous preacher of the age, very much like Billy Graham in the late 20th century. Born in the Berkshire Mountain village of Northfield, Massachusetts, Moody moved to Chicago as a young man and soon mastered the shoe business. But a conversion experience turned his attention from business to religion. Although he never received ordination, he put his considerable organizational abilities to the Lord's use by starting a church, launching Sunday schools, and supporting the work of the newly formed Young Men's Christian Association (YMCA). By the 1870s Moody and his song leader, Ira Sankey, were preaching all across the northern and midwestern United States and even in Britain.

Moody won the affection of millions for a number of reasons. One was his preaching style. In it he avoided technical theological discussions. He focused upon what he called the three Rs: ruin by sin, redemption by Christ, and regeneration by the Holy Spirit. Rarely speaking of hell, Moody stressed instead God's love for all. He told homey, sentimental stories about sinners falling upon hard times until they gave their lives to Christ—unless of course they waited until it was too late and perished for their sins. All this took place against a backdrop of stirring revival tunes adroitly led by Sankey.

Critics sometimes groused that Moody possessed little formal education, but they failed to see that he was no bumpkin. His simple words

carried profound messages. Keenly aware that a visible commitment would be hard to abandon, Moody urged his hearers to step forward and give their lives to Christ in public. He carefully secured the support of a broad spectrum of local pastors before entering a city, thus creating the impression that he spoke for the community at large. And he took care to institutionalize his message after he departed. Moody founded schools for young women and young men in his home town of Northfield and a Bible training school in Chicago for students too poor to go to college. After his death trustees renamed it Moody Bible Institute. (It was to thrive in the 20th century as one of the wealthiest, strongest, most prestigious of the conservative Protestant colleges.)

If Moody focused upon winning men and women to Christ, other evangelists tried to help converts nurture a vigorous Christian life after conversion. Their aim was to have converts love Christ so completely that they would never desire to sin again. This emphasis on spiritual growth went by various names: sanctification, holiness, second blessing, consecration, higher Christian life, or Holy Spirit baptism. By whatever label, the movement washed across thousands of evangelical groups, white and black, north and south. It waxed strongest among the Methodists, from whose ranks emerged several small but influential sects, including the Salvation Army and the Church of the Nazarene.

Dwight L. Moody (standing, left) and Ira Sankey (standing, right) held campaigns of Christian conversion in Brooklyn, New York, and across the nation. The pair inspired thousands of converts in the United States as well as Britain.

Phoebe Palmer's magazine, *Guide to Holiness,* offered readers spiritual growth by means of sanctification, or purification, through the truth of God. One of the banners on the cover sums up this idea: "Sanctify them through thy truth. Thy word is truth."

No one did more to stir a desire for sanctification than Phoebe Palmer. The wife of a wealthy New York physician, Palmer pressed Christians to trust Christ's promise that all residues of sin could be removed and replaced with a single-hearted love for God and others. She expressed her ideas in best-selling books, in a steady stream of articles in her monthly magazine, *Guide to Holiness,* and in sermons preached on both sides of the Atlantic. Under her ministry, which spanned the middle third of the century, hundreds of thousands, perhaps millions, professed sanctification. Contrary to popular stereotypes about women preachers, Palmer was tough minded and clear eyed. Although she esteemed deep emotion as a desirable fruit of conversion and of Holy Spirit baptism (as she usually called it), she insisted that the initial commitment to Christ was a rational process of first believing the Bible's promises, then acting upon them.

Sanctification's advocates distinguished themselves in several ways. They championed missions, both at home and abroad, especially among the humbler classes. Although they rarely involved themselves in secular politics, they urged well-fed, middle-class Christians to take off their gloves and help the down and out, especially in the squalid cities. They spent considerable time establishing and working in urban rescue missions, such as Jerry McAuley's famed Water Street Mission in New York's Bowery district. They insisted that women be allowed to preach (though not necessarily ordained). And they called for strict standards of personal conduct, sharply condemning smoking, drinking, dancing, gambling, and sex outside of marriage. These restrictions emerged from a

Phoebe Palmer's Religious Feminism

Phoebe Palmer, editor of Guide to Holiness *(1864–74), one of the most influential religious periodicals of the 19th century, did not think of herself as a crusading feminist. Yet she insisted that women should be encouraged to speak publicly about matters of faith and morals. In* The Promise of the Father *(1859) Palmer argued that the customs of the churches must give way to the plain teachings of the Bible and Christ's will.*

What is meant by preaching the gospel? Says the devoted Dr. Wayland [a well-known Baptist theologian]: . . . "The words translated [as] preach in our version are two. The one signifies, simply, to herald, to announce, to proclaim, to publish. The other, with this general idea, combines the notion of good tidings, and means to publish, or be the messenger of good news.". . . And if this be the scriptural meaning of the word preach, then where is the Christian, either of the clergy or laity, but would have every man, woman, or child, who had an experiential knowledge of the saving power of Christ, herald far and near the tidings of a Saviour willing and able to save? . . .

But the well-known fact, that earnestly-pious and intelligent women are ever withstood, and the testimony of their lips ruled out, with but few exceptions, in the presence of the men, in nearly all church communities, seems of itself more like a return to barbarism than a perpetuation of Christianity.

conviction that such conduct undermined social stability and wrecked personal happiness.

The emphasis upon spiritual growth and personal uprightness that swept across evangelical Protestantism at the end of the 19th century challenged men more directly than women. Respectable middle-class men and women of the late 19th century quietly assumed that women most properly served God as wives and mothers. As such they were supposed to stay home and guard the moral purity of the household. Men, on the other hand, were expected to achieve success in the rough-and-tumble world of business, industry, and finance. Very few conservative Protestants openly endorsed the idea of men breaking the rules, let alone living immoral lives, but sometimes it seemed necessary to stretch the rules a bit in order to make a dollar. Sanctification's adherents tolerated none of that. Like fiery Old Testament prophets, they denounced all expressions of the double standard.

The desire to conserve the best of historic Christianity took still another form—one that persists with great force today. After the Civil War, millions of earnest Americans came to believe that the Bible taught that Christ would soon return to the earth in literal, physical form. Partisans of this view called themselves premillennialists. (This term meant that Christ would come back before the millennium, the thousand years of peace and righteousness that, according to the New Testament, would mark the end of history.) Though premillennialist beliefs had cropped up only rarely in the long history of Christianity, in North America in the late 19th century they gained broad appeal. The Seventh-day Adventists, an offshoot of the mid-century Millerites discussed earlier, formed one prominent example. Like the Millerites, the Adventists eagerly anticipated Christ's visible Advent, or Second Coming, but unlike the Millerites they did not set precise dates. We shall return to the Adventists' story later in the context of diet and health, which they linked to end-time preparations.

The waning years of the century saw the birth of another premillennialist group that became a household name after World War II. These believers, now called Jehovah's Witnesses, originally labeled themselves Russellites after their founder, Charles Taze Russell. Born in 1852, this thoughtful, energetic leader grew up in a Presbyterian household near Pittsburgh. Russell left school early to run his family's clothing business while studying the Bible intensively on his own. His Zion's Watch Tower Society, which he organized in 1884, heralded beliefs measurably different from those of most Christians. For one thing, hell did not exist. Neither did the Trinity (Father, Son, Holy Spirit). Instead, God, properly known by his Old Testament name, Jehovah, reigned alone. Christ existed as a divine though lesser being. Russell maintained that Christ had returned to earth in spirit in 1874. Soon Jehovah, along with Christ and the Holy Angels, would launch a terrible war upon Satan and his followers. Jehovah's victory over Satan would be followed by a thousand years free of poverty, suffering, and injustice, including racial injustice.

The beliefs of Charles Taze Russell, shown here in his study, appealed to many who felt the injustices of poverty and racism in the late 19th century. His followers, called Russellites, are now called Jehovah's Witnesses.

In the meantime, Russell taught, the Jehovah's Witnesses must keep themselves pure by not smoking, drinking, or associating with the government in any form. Russell believed that government, most businesses, and the traditional Christian churches oppressed the poor and needy even as they increased the wealth and power of the wicked. This meant of course that Witnesses should not fight in the country's wars. It also meant refusing to salute the flag, which aroused the ire of their neighbors. Nonetheless, Russell's controversial ideas proved to be appealing. One early book sold 5 million copies, and all of his writings together sold 15 million copies in 30 languages.

Fundamentalists represented by far the largest, most influential cluster of believers concerned about Christ's second coming. These believers did not acquire the name *fundamentalists* until the 1920s. But the label was a good one, even in the 1870s, because they fervently believed that the promise that Christ would soon return formed one of the fundamental teachings of the Bible. Fundamentalists did not possess a single dominant leader, but hundreds of forceful men and women took up the cause. They supposed that every word of the Bible, rightly translated and interpreted, was factually true. Working from that assumption, most fundamentalists divided history into distinct eras, usually seven. By their reckoning history was nearing the end of the sixth era. Soon, they taught, Christ would come back to earth, defeat Satan, then launch a thousand years of peace and righteousness. They called this seventh era of human history, when Christ alone would reign, the millennium. At the end of the millennium, God would judge all humans, living and dead, sending the righteous to everlasting heaven and the evil to eternal hell.

Why did these notions, supposedly so much out of step with the secular trends of the age, seem so persuasive to millions of Americans? Several answers come to mind. For one thing, the movement was blessed with gifted leaders who built a nationwide network of schools, colleges, and periodicals. These leaders pressed their ideas in summer Bible conferences, boosted by the spread of railroads and the growing popularity of summer vacations. Moreover, fundamentalists seemed to offer a credible explanation for the trend of world events. Look around, they urged. What do you see? War, greed, and sexual immorality. Surely God's patience must be wearing thin and he would bring history to an end very soon. Above all, millions found joy in the prospect that Christ, whom they loved, would soon come back to earth. Not surprisingly, they called that prospect the Blessed Hope.

Other Protestants found security in the traditions of their particular denominational traditions or ethnic groups. None proved as visible to the broader public as the groups we have been discussing, but they won thousands of adherents, and most continued to flourish in the late 20th century. The Churches of Christ, best known perhaps for their refusal to allow pianos or musical instruments in their worship services, illustrated the trend. Their story goes back to the Christians/Disciples of Christ who emerged before the Civil War. The Disciples aimed to restore the simplicity of New Testament patterns of belief and worship, discarding complex confessions and theologies. After the Civil War they increasingly accepted modern values, such as biblical higher criticism (indeed, many of the most prominent liberals were Disciples). Near the turn of the century a large minority of Disciples pulled away from the larger body, calling for a return to simple New Testament standards. They called their gatherings churches of Christ (*churches* was spelled with a lowercase *c* to make clear that they were individual churches, not a new sect).

Members of the churches of Christ were not really evangelicals, for they did not encourage emotional conversion experiences. But they insisted that the Bible must be read rationally and obeyed strictly, because it was true in all respects. Churches of Christ flourished everywhere, especially in the Upper South states of Tennessee, Missouri, Arkansas, Oklahoma, and Texas.

Another large family of Christians, loosely called the Peace Churches, also marked American religious life at the end of the century. The Peace Churches consisted of two large branches, the Quakers and the Mennonites. The Quakers stemmed from the English Reformation in the 17th century, the Mennonites from the Reformation in continental Europe in the 16th century. Both had put down roots in the United States long before the American Revolution, clustering in eastern Pennsylvania, where they enjoyed freedom from persecution. By the late 19th century both could be found almost everywhere, although they remained strongest in Pennsylvania and later in the central Midwest.

In America Quakers and Mennonites followed parallel theological paths. After the Civil War the majority of Quakers embraced liberal religious attitudes, but a large minority continued to emphasize traditional ideals of pacifism and a simple lifestyle. Most Mennonites, including the Mennonite offshoots of the Amish and the Brethren in Christ, did the same. All these groups suffered severe persecution for refusing to fight in World War I. Though never large in numbers, they loomed large in the popular imagination. Their stance provided other Americans with a compelling example of what it meant to take one's faith seriously, whatever the cost.

The leopard with the harmless kid laid down
And not one savage beast was seen to frown

The wolf did with the lambkin dwell in peace
His grim carnivorous nature there did cease

The lion with the fatling on did move
A little child was leading them in love;

When the great PENN his famous treaty made
With indian chiefs beneath the Elm-tree's shade.

This 1826 painting by Edward Hicks emphasizes the pacifist beliefs of the Quakers. It shows predatory animals side by side with their prey, as well as the famous treaty of 1681 between the Quaker William Penn and the Indians of Pennsylvania.

Another expression of tradition flowered on the Iowa prairie and the eastern shore of Lake Michigan in the latter half of the century. These earnest, hardworking believers were the Dutch Reformed, Calvinists who had emigrated to the United States from the Netherlands in the early 19th century. In the United States they split into the Reformed Church in America and the more conservative Christian Reformed Church. Members of the latter, especially, kept to themselves, carefully charting their lives by the creeds of the Protestant Reformation. Strict observers of the Sunday sabbath, they enjoyed their cigars no less than their tulip gardens. They made a lasting mark upon U.S. education by erecting a private school system second to none and by cultivating distinguished scholars in theology, philosophy, and history.

We do not have to look to the smaller groups on the margins of the culture to see tradition at work. Many believers in the large, well-established denominations also found their primary identity in the heritage of the past. One of the most conspicuous examples emerged among the Episcopalians. Calling themselves High Church Episcopalians, these Christians emphasized ancient creeds. They relished elaborate liturgies resembling the practices of the Church of England in the age of King James I. Some even adopted processions, incense, and the use of bells in worship. Inspired by the art and architecture of European Christianity, they built lovely Georgian, Romanesque, and Gothic churches and cathedrals. Many of those structures, such as Trinity Church in lower Manhattan and Trinity Church in the heart of Boston, continue to grace U.S. skylines.

Memories of the past strongly shaped the Lutheran experience in America too. The first Lutherans emigrated from Sweden in the early 17th century to settle in lower New York and upper Delaware. But they remained small in number until after the Civil War, when their ranks swelled rapidly with newcomers from Germany and Scandinavia. Claiming one-half million followers in 1870, Lutheran rolls swelled to 2 million in 1910, making them the fourth-largest Christian denominational family.

The Lutherans had a hard time working with each other. They spoke multiple languages, including German, Danish, Norwegian, Swedish, Finnish, and Icelandic. Moreover, they often lived on farms or in tight-knit rural communities very much like the fictional Lake Wobegone in Garrison Keillor's "Prairie Home Companion" books and radio shows. This settlement pattern reduced the need for interaction with other Lutheran ethnic groups. Nonetheless, in the end Lutherans tried to embrace common historic traditions in the continental Reformation rather than modern America for a shared point of reference.

Looking to the Old World for spiritual guidance was, however, easier said than done. Again, Lutherans differed among themselves. The sharply contrasting outlooks of two leaders, Samuel Simon Schmucker and C. F. W. Walther, illustrate the problem. Their lives spanned the first three-quarters of the century. Both gained a wide reputation for piety, learning, and commitment to Lutheran success in America. Both founded

Trinity Church in New York City, as it appeared in 1847, was built in the Gothic Revival style, which is based on the church architecture of the Middle Ages in Europe. The church still stands today, but it is surrounded by skyscrapers.

important schools. And each felt that the historic confessions of the church, especially the Augsburg Confession of 1530, accurately summarized the Bible's main teachings. But there their paths separated. Schmucker wanted Lutheran worship to be less liturgical and spoken in English. Like most American Protestants he supported temperance (no alcohol) and strict sabbath observance. He also urged cooperation with other Protestants in missions and Sunday schools.

Walther, on the other hand, opposed all these moves. Because the true faith had flourished in the Old World, he saw no reason to accommodate U.S. patterns. With great determination Walther insisted that Lutherans needed to uphold all the doctrines summarized in the historic confessions of the church. Nor was English an adequate substitute for the purity of the German tongue.

In the end Schmucker lost and Walther won. The majority of Lutherans felt that Schmucker gave away too much. Walther expected sacrifice, and ordinary people took pride in their ability to stand the test. Sometimes Americans clung to marginalized traditions precisely because it was the most difficult thing to do.

The effort to find hope for the present in the traditions of the past extended beyond Protestants, beyond Christians, beyond Jews. The Native Americans too looked back—but with a difference. If European Americans used religion to make life better and more meaningful, Native Americans used it to make life possible.

On several occasions in the 18th and 19th centuries American Indian prophets had called their people to embrace the ways of the distant past in order to find the resources, both material and spiritual, to expel whites from their lands. About 1800, for example, Handsome Lake led a revitalization movement, as outsiders later called it, among his Seneca people in upstate New York. The movement stemmed from instructions Lake said he had received during a heavenly journey. These directions banned alcohol, witchcraft, and abortion. The Shawnee Indian Tenskwatawa and his brother Tecumtha (or Tecumseh) led a similar stirring in the middle years of the 19th century. They too banned liquor and witchcraft, as well as intermarriage with whites. Tenskwatawa's influence centered in Ohio but spread from Florida to Saskatchewan.

The Ghost Dance, inspired by a Nevada Paiute Indian named Wovoka, produced one of the most widespread expressions of tradition-based Native American religion. During the winter of 1888–89 Wovoka, then a young man of 32, dreamed that he was taken up into a heavenly realm of green grasses and abundant game. The Indian dead of ages past, now restored to robust strength, populated the realm. There Wovoka received instructions for his people. They were to give up warfare with each other and with whites. He learned of a special dance that would hasten the day when whites would disappear from the land, the earth would be restored to its original beauty, and Indians would be reunited with their bygone ancestors. Wovoka's message quickly spread eastward across the Great Plains.

In the 1880s the Oglala Sioux, one of the most warlike plains tribes, adopted and adapted the doctrine to their own needs. The Sioux believed that the special dance, performed with long white shirts painted with red symbols, would make them bulletproof. This notion fueled a series of confrontations with federal soldiers. In the end, 200 Sioux were slain at Wounded Knee, South Dakota, in the cold winter of 1890. The songs and rituals of the ceremony soon faded into local practices. Other forms of Indian religion, along with Indian Christianity, would see a powerful rebirth in the late 20th century. But the soul of the Ghost Dance, like much of Native American culture, died on the windswept plains of the West. Even tradition had its limits.

Chapter 10

Adventurers

Onward, Christian soldiers, marching as to war,
with the cross of Jesus going on before,
Christ, the royal Master, leads against the foe;
forward into battle see his banners go!
　　—*Sabine Baring-Gould, "Onward, Christian Soldiers" (1864)*

As the 19th century drew to a close, religious men and women everywhere reached out to embrace the world and transform it in positive ways: adventurers of the spirit, we might call them. Just as religious ideals had energized visionary reformers before the Civil War, so too did they energize farsighted souls two generations later. But this time there was a difference. In the intervening 50 years the nation itself had changed, in fundamental ways. The extremes of wealth and poverty had widened. Class suspicions had sharpened. Farmers' lives had grown more risky economically. Blacks' new freedom had stirred whites' fears. Technology had opened the non-Western world to Western involvement. Religious citizens responded to these challenges in a wide variety of ways, some effective, others less so. But respond they did. Americans had many sins, but indifference was rarely one of them.

Four efforts to reach out and change the world for the better stand out above the others. These attempts included new ideas about the care of the human body, the easing of poverty in the nation's swelling cities, the reduction of the suffering caused by alcohol abuse, and the vast effort to Christianize and aid people in other lands. In the 1880s and 1890s

Bishop William T. Vernon and his wife, Emily E. Vernon, rest on a mission in South Africa in the early 20th century. They belonged to the African Methodist Episcopal (A.M.E.) church.

reformers targeted many additional evils, including prostitution, the misuse of the sabbath, and the repression of women. However, health, poverty, alcohol, and missions took precedence.

The concern for health was an old story. All Western religions, including Judaism and Christianity, had much to say about the care of the human body. But the terrible carnage of the Civil War, plus new ideas in the late 19th century about how to improve and even lengthen human life, prompted believers to think about the relation between religion and health in creative ways.

Three distinctly different health efforts marked the religious landscape. The first was divine healing. This trend proved to be especially strong among radical evangelicals—mostly individuals with Baptist or Methodist backgrounds notable for their fierce independence and stormy preaching. Radical evangelicals assumed that sin produced physical suffering. Thus, they argued that when Jesus promised to bear away the sins of the world, he also promised to bear away suffering. "Only Trust Him" said a popular hymn, only trust that Christ would do what he promised to do.

Divine healing prompted the formation of several sects specially committed to the practice. Best known perhaps was the Christian and Missionary Alliance, which emerged in the 1880s and soon spread around the world. The idea of healing through Christ also undergirded the Pentecostal revival, which arose just after the turn of the 20th century. (Pentecostals took their name from the Day of Pentecost when, according to the New Testament, Christians miraculously spoke languages they had never learned.) Following World War II, television evangelists like Oral Roberts and Kathryn Kuhlman helped make Pentecostalism the largest new Christian movement of the 20th century.

A second healing movement stemmed from the teachings of Ellen G. White. In the 1850s White joined the remnants of the Millerites, who had predicted Christ's return in 1844. She first led the crestfallen believers into Saturday worship (prompted by powerful dream visions), then into strong interest in the care of the physical body (also prompted by visions). White reminded her followers that the body remained the temple of the Lord. Declaring that people made "a god of their bellies," Adventists paid close attention to what people should and should not eat. They opposed eating any form of meat, especially red meat, swine's flesh (ham), and shellfish like shrimp. They urged people to avoid cooking vegetables with lard and salt in favor of steaming and eating them with scarcely any seasoning. Realizing that people would find such a diet unattractive, Adventists invented tasty substitutes, including cold breakfast cereals. Battle Creek, Michigan, their headquarters, became synonymous with cornflakes, created by Adventist leader John Harvey Kellogg.

Spurred by White, Adventists urged additional health reforms. These included hard beds, regular exercise, sunshine, fresh air, frequent bathing in warm mineral waters, avoidance of alcohol and tobacco, and safer, more comfortable clothing for women (thus doing away with corsets and high heels). Adventists denounced undue sex within marriage. They scorned physicians and the use of chemical drugs. Some of their health reforms received mixed support at the time but enjoyed wide approval—often for different reasons—later on. In time the Adventists established colleges, universities, orphanages, and state-of-the-art hospitals belting the globe. Loma Linda University Medical Center in California ranked among the finest medical research institutions anywhere.

A third health-focused movement, commonly called Christian Science, emerged from the genius of Mary Baker Eddy. This forceful though somewhat mysterious woman was born in New Hampshire in 1821. She suffered from depression, economic insecurity, an unhappy marriage, and constant ill health throughout her young adulthood. In desperation Eddy dabbled in hypnotism and water cures, which in those days were a common remedy entailing frequent "flushing" of the body's system. A

The first design for the box of Kellogg's Corn Flakes in 1906 included the signature of W. K. Kellogg, Dr. John Harvey Kellogg's brother. Dr. Kellogg refused to make money from his cereal, which had been invented only as a health product, so his brother formed the Kellogg's Company on his own.

Mary Baker Eddy Stresses Mind Over Matter

In Rudimental Divine Science (1891) and in No and Yes (1891), Christian Science founder Mary Baker Eddy struggled to make clear to uncomprehending Americans that God was an Idea and that the world—which came from God—also was an Idea. Therefore, matter was an illusion and disease and death were lies, albeit terrible ones.

To Mary Baker Eddy, sin, suffering, and illness were imaginary, since God's perfect mind would not allow such flaws to exist. Eddy's Christian Scientists strove to preserve their health by denying these illusions through the study of God.

What is the Principle of Christian Science? It is God, the Supreme Being, infinite and immortal Mind, the Soul of man and the universe. It is our Father which is in heaven. It is substance, Spirit, Life, Truth, and Love,—these are the deific Principle. . . .

Is there no matter? All is Mind. . . . The five material senses testify to the existence of matter. The spiritual senses afford no such evidence, but deny the testimony of the material senses. . . .

Disease is more than imagination; it is a human error, a constituent part of what comprise[s] the whole of mortal existence,—material sensation and mental delusion. . . . [T]he Science of Mind-healing destroys the feasibility of disease; hence error of thought becomes fable instead of fact. . . .

Is healing the sick the whole of Science? Healing physical sickness is the smallest part of Christian Science. It is only the bugle-call to thought and action. . . . The emphatic purpose of Christian Science is the healing of sin; and this task, sometimes, may be harder than the cure of disease; because, while mortals love to sin, they do not love to be sick.

New England folk healer named Phineas P. Quimby finally helped her find relief. Quimby taught Eddy that all reality was simply an idea in God's mind. Because God's pure and perfect mind could hold no error, let alone suffering or death, the unhappy facts of everyday life were in fact illusions. Eddy adopted and elaborated these notions. She argued that a truly modern or scientific understanding of Jesus Christ would see him not as a divine being but rather as a human who understood that material things as well as sin, error, and illness existed only in the dark recesses of the human imagination.

Eddy's teachings found particular favor in the Boston area. There, in the historic citadel of Puritans, Unitarians, and Transcendentalists, she founded the Massachusetts Metaphysical College in 1881. That institution eventually grew into one of the wealthiest and most influential sects in the United States: the Church of Christ, Scientist. Christian Scientists, as its partisans called themselves, did not endorse preachers. Instead, worship was led by "readers" or "practitioners" who read from the Bible and from Eddy's main writing, *Science and Health, with Key to the Scriptures* (1875). These men and women helped converts preserve their health by seeing the illusion of matter, error, and illness. Drugs—including tobacco, alcohol, and sometimes caffeine—clouded the mind's ability to see the truth. Perhaps more than any other religious tradition in America, Christian Science proved to be congenial to middle- and upper-middle-class women. Though never large (by 1910, at Eddy's death, the church's membership had reached only 100,000), Eddy's teachings nonetheless strongly appealed to the wealthy and well educated.

Unfortunately, America's cities harbored millions who were neither wealthy nor well educated. While the population of the nation tripled between 1880 and 1910, the number in the cities grew thirtyfold. Millions abandoned farms, especially in the South, for better-paying jobs in the cities. And millions more swept through the port cities, in a vast migration from eastern and southern Europe and, to a lesser extent, from Asia as well. Though many found opportunities unknown in their previous lives, others (perhaps a majority) encountered 12-hour days, six-day work weeks, and the constant danger of loss of limb in the fast-moving machinery of the factories. Newcomers found themselves jammed into tenement houses, entire families living in a single room without plumbing or adequate heat or ventilation.

Humane souls of all sorts rose to the challenge, Christian and Jew, Protestant and Catholic. In retrospect two of those many efforts to ease the squalor and suffering in the cities particularly stand out. One was called the Social Gospel, the other the Salvation Army.

Earlier efforts by British Protestants to ease the pain of the urban poor, especially in London, influenced the American Social Gospelers. The latter believed that most Christians spent too much time trying to save the soul and not enough saving the body. The Social Gospelers thus established a string of churches in the urban Northeast, often called institutional churches, that offered a variety of social services, including health care, help in finding jobs, and recreational facilities. Starting in the 1870s, Washington Gladden, a Congregational pastor in Columbus, Ohio, wrote 30 books and hundreds of articles challenging wealthy Christians to search their consciences. He especially urged business owners to give laborers a living wage. At a time when 10 percent of the nation's families had cornered 70 percent of the nation's wealth, it seemed high time for decent, God-fearing folk to ask themselves what was fair.

The answers were not long in coming. *In His Steps,* an 1897 novel written by a Topeka, Kansas, Congregational minister named Charles M. Sheldon responded to this question without flinching. This popular book, one of the best-selling American novels of the 19th century, portrayed the dilemmas that typical Americans would face if every time they faced an ethical decision they honestly asked themselves a single, disturbing question: "What would Jesus do?" Later on, especially after the turn of the century, the Social Gospelers promoted more concrete solutions to urban ills. They urged state and federal governments to step in and force employers to limit the working day to ten (and later eight) hours, to guarantee a day of rest each week, to keep children out of the mines and away from dangerous machinery, and to provide at least minimal health and sanitation facilities.

These solutions resembled proposals advanced by labor unions such as the Knights of Labor. But there was a difference. The Social Gospelers armed themselves with the teachings of the Hebrew prophets and the example of Jesus. The Bible, they insisted, never presented the gospel as good news for individuals alone. True biblical faith aimed to redeem society too.

The Salvation Army spearheaded another major effort to meet the urban challenge. Founded in London in the 1860s by Methodists William and Catherine Booth, the Army arrived in the United States, horns blowing, in 1880. In the United States the Army found its main supporters among radical evangelicals, especially those with Methodist roots. After the turn of the century the Booths' flamboyant, strong-willed daughter, Evangeline, ran the U.S. operation with the efficiency of a well-oiled machine. Dressed in their distinctive uniforms, caps, and bonnets, the Army's corporals and captains—male and female alike—aided the urban poor in many ways. They provided low-cost coal in winter and ice in summer. They distributed free food and medicine to the destitute and hungry. They sheltered orphans and unwed mothers. They fashioned education and training programs to help the penniless break the cycle of poverty. They helped alcoholics kick the habit and find productive work.

The Social Gospelers and the Salvation Army's workers sought similar goals. They both wanted people, especially the poor, to be treated fairly, to receive a living wage, to enjoy the benefits of clean housing and good medical care. But their approaches differed. The Social Gospelers increasingly looked toward long-range solutions, involving labor unions,

Charles Sheldon's book *In His Steps* (1897) was so popular that it was the basis for a 1970s comic book that urged teenagers to consider what Jesus would do in a situation before acting themselves.

The Salvation Army made a special effort to meet the needs of city dwellers, especially the poor. Here, Salvation Army workers, in their distinctive hats, comfort and guide members of an urban congregation, including both blacks and whites.

laws and regulations, and the enforcing power of the state. The Army, on the other hand, looked toward more immediate solutions, helping the unemployed laborer next door find a meal this morning and a job this afternoon. It was a perennial dilemma. Should Christians try to solve the underlying causes of poverty? Or should they concentrate on the suffering at hand? Neither movement showed much interest in the main reform causes of the late 20th century, equality for minorities and for women. But both proved that biblical faith carried within itself powerful forces for the social as well as spiritual redemption of the cities.

Reforming the cities meant reforming Americans' misuse of alcohol. For the better part of a century, from the 1820s through the 1920s, religious men and women increasingly turned their attention to the harmful effects of excessive drinking. Although many antebellum abolitionists had championed temperance—Jonathan Blanchard, the first president of Wheaton College in Illinois comes to mind—the four decades flanking the turn of the 20th century marked the high point of that crusade. In colonial America, Christians had never endorsed drunkenness, yet they seemed rather lax about enforcing sobriety. Weddings involved considerable drinking, especially in the Anglican South and sometimes in the Puritan North.

In the early 19th century the quantity of drinking grew, with the typical adult male consuming an average of a half-pint of hard liquor each day. But at the same time, with the coming of industrialization and its attendant need for punctuality and carefulness around machinery, the demand for sobriety also grew. Thus in the 1840s Maine and Massachusetts passed laws against the production of hard liquor. These prohibitions did not last long, old consumption habits being hard to break, but they prefigured bigger things to come.

The real push for temperance emerged in the 1880s. Before the Civil War, temperance meant exactly what the word suggested: moderation. But eventually it came to mean abstinence: drinking no alcohol at all, not even medicinally. Reformers assumed that one drink led to another. The cause united men and women across the religious and political spectrums. They commonly worried about the sinister effects of drunkenness upon the home and the workplace. They labored together to pass laws to stop the production and sale of alcohol. They also worked together to create the unspoken expectation that sobriety was good and drunkenness disgraceful. The point was less to make intoxication illegal than to make it unthinkable. But making it illegal helped. In 1919 a broad coalition of religious groups persuaded Congress to pass the Eighteenth Amendment to the Constitution, prohibiting the sale of alcoholic beverages anywhere in the United States. Fourteen years later, in the face of widespread flouting of the law, Congress reversed itself and passed the Twenty-first Amendment, abolishing the Eighteenth.

Who supported temperance and who opposed it? Its main adherents included English-speaking Protestants, especially Methodists and Baptists, north and south, and a number of Irish Catholic leaders concerned about the perils of drinking among workers. The opposers included continental Protestants and Catholics, especially Germans, who clung to Old

World folkways. They also included the lower and upper classes of all (and no) religious persuasions, who saw temperance as an effort by middle-class do-gooders to run other people's lives.

And then there were the women who saw drink as part of a larger complex of social ills. No one did more to curb alcohol abuse than Frances Willard. This earnest crusader grew up near Chicago in a Methodist home, an affiliation she retained to the end of her days. As an instructor in the women's college of Northwestern University, Willard advocated equal opportunities for women in higher education. But her concern about the harmful effects of alcohol upon the home drew her into the newly formed Women's Christian Temperance Union, better known as the WCTU. Willard's business skills soon propelled her to the presidency of that organization. For the three decades from the 1880s to 1910 she tirelessly crisscrossed the United States, calling for self-discipline for the willing, temperance laws for the unwilling.

Willard's reforming instincts ranged widely. In her mind, drunkenness persisted as one of many closely linked social problems, including, most notably, the sorry status of women. After the Civil War, middle-class women found themselves increasingly restricted to the home or to the company of other women outside the home. They were supposed to protect the morals of the family but not enter the public workplace. Willard was no radical. She did not seek to overturn the basic gender roles. But she forcefully agitated for woman suffrage—the right to vote—and for a woman's right to enter into business or political life if she wished.

Frances Willard also attacked prostitution and the abusive treatment of children. Ironically, perhaps, her crusade for woman suffrage, social purity (anti-prostitution), and child protection laws would see more success in constitutional amendments and federal and state legislation in the 20th century than would her concern for alcohol abuse.

By any reasonable measure of such things, the most spectacular religious adventure of the late 19th century started in the United States but ended far away, on countless mission fields overseas. To be sure, some groups never caught the spirit. The Jews and Lutherans, for example,

Woman's Christian Temperance Union of Pennsylvania

For God and Home and Native Land

PLEDGE

I hereby solemnly promise, God helping me, to abstain from all distilled, fermented and malt liquors, including wine, beer and cider, as a beverage, and to employ all proper means to discourage the use of, and traffic in the same.

Name ....

Name ....

Address ....

Dues Paid ....

This Coupon for Secretary.

Signer of Pledge retains card.

remained more interested in nurturing their faith among their own children, generation after generation, than in extending it to outsiders. And some caught it late. Although U.S. Catholics launched the Maryknoll Missioners in 1908, until the 20th century they had to work hard just to survive in an unfriendly environment. All of this is to say that the older English-speaking denominations—Congregationalists, Presbyterians, Methodists, and Baptists—served as the main carriers of the missionary vision in 19th-century America.

Domestic missions to Native Americans came first. One of the most conspicuous efforts involved the mission to the Cherokees, historically clustered in the southern highlands. By the 1820s, when Andrew Jackson became President, the Cherokees had already moved far toward Christianity, unlike most Indian groups. Even so, their grim fate was settled when whites discovered gold in the Georgia hills. Despite treaties guaranteeing the natives' right to stay, in the 1830s Jackson forcibly marched them along the Trail of Tears to the Oklahoma Territory. In the meantime, though, numbers of missionaries had grown deeply to respect the Cherokees' integrity and way of life, Christian or not. Some, such as Evan Jones and his son John B. Jones, both Baptists, struggled alongside the

When a woman joined the WCTU, she filled out a stub, like the one here, for her membership, and carried the card as a reminder of her pledge. The picture is of Frances Willard, an early member and president of the union.

Missionary Eliza Spalding made this six-foot-long chart to help the Indians of Oregon learn Christian history. On the right is the path to heaven and on the left, the wider path of damnation.

Indians against the federal forces. In the end, everyone lost. The Cherokees lost their homes, the missionaries their credibility, and the federal government its honor.

After the Civil War the missionary spirit targeted another evil: white racism and its stepchild, black poverty. Concern about the treatment of blacks had preceded the Civil War. It stirred the conscience of reform-minded sects like the Quakers and Free Methodists, prompted the formation of abolitionist societies, and helped spark the war itself. But if the Thirteenth Amendment (passed in 1865) abolished slavery, white racism persisted in other forms. In the late 1870s, for example, the federal government withdrew troops from the South. This move allowed Southerners to pass regulations, called Jim Crow laws, that required blacks to go to separate schools and avoid informal contact with whites on trains, in restaurants, or in public parks. Also, blacks' inability to find fair-paying jobs drove many into sharecropping, making it virtually impossible for them to gain any measure of economic independence. At the same time, whites displayed growing fear of black males. Some accounts held that the South witnessed three lynchings per week through the 1890s.

Both white and black Christians responded to these abuses. After the war, Northern white denominations sent hundreds of missionaries southward to build schools and orphanages and to distribute food and medical supplies. Many of these volunteers were women. The American Missionary Association, formed in 1846, focused upon educating freed slaves. Leading black colleges and universities, including Fisk, Hampton, Morehouse, Talladega, and Tougaloo, grew from such efforts.

Black Christians shouldered the burden too. Despite daunting obstacles they established Lane, Livingstone, Paul Quinn, and Morris Brown colleges, among others. They published books and newspapers (the A.M.E.Z.'s twice monthly *Star of Zion*, published in the South almost continually since 1877, ranks as one of the oldest religious papers in the United States). Under the leadership of activists like A.M.E. Bishop Henry

Pearl Sydenstricker (far right) grew up in China with her evangelist parents in the late 19th century. Later, distancing herself from the missionary cause, she too lived and taught in China. As Pearl S. Buck, she used her experiences there in her books, and was the first woman to win a Nobel Prize for Literature.

McNeal Turner, they launched sustained efforts for the colonization of blacks in Africa as an alternative to the brutality of white racism at home.

And then, finally, there is the story of the foreign mission enterprise itself. This venture remains one of the great tales of U.S. religious history, filled with the feats of saints and heroes and, sad to say, the misdeeds of one or two scoundrels as well. Numerical data have to be used carefully, but they at least give us some idea of the size of the missionary effort of those years. Though a steady stream of Americans had been going abroad as missionaries ever since 1812, as late as 1890 fewer than a thousand lived overseas. By the turn of the century, however, that number had swollen to 5,000, which constituted a quarter of all the Christian missionaries in the world. (Twenty-five years later U.S. missionaries would constitute nearly half of the global total.) In 1886 evangelist Dwight L. Moody founded the Student Volunteer Movement, soon better known as the SVM. In the next 50 years the SVM stirred the imagination and touched the hearts of tens of thousands of young men and women. At least 13,000 actually sailed for far-off lands. A solid majority, perhaps 60 percent, of all U.S. missionaries were women.

Sometimes missionaries received support from their parent denominations. Starting in the 1880s, however, many who called themselves "faith" missionaries left without any initial promise of support. Independent organizations with exotic-sounding names like the Africa Inland Mission and the Sudan Interior Mission sent them to the remotest parts of the globe.

In the course of the 19th century U.S. missionaries fanned out literally all over the world. They won the Sandwich Islands (Hawaii) to Christianity by mid-century. Missions to Africa started in the 1820s. Spurred primarily by free blacks in the United States, missions in Africa grew steadily as European powers partitioned the continent piece by piece. In the later years of the century the majority of Protestant emissaries focused their attention upon Southeast Asia, especially China. Most tried primarily to win nonbelievers to the Christian faith, but in the process they also built hundreds of schools, hospitals, and orphanages. They mapped the landscape, measured volcanic eruptions, studied native plants and animals, reduced unwritten languages to written form, and translated the Bible into the vernacular languages of the local peoples. Often they did the reverse too: translating obscure languages into English. Missionaries were in some cases the first to render remote languages into *any* written form. In the Belgian Congo in the 1890s the Protestant missionaries were the first to codify in written form the Longkundo dialect, for instance.

All these trends—determination, brains, courage—manifested themselves in the lives of one particularly gifted and particularly famous missionary family, Adoniram Judson and his three successive wives. Just out of seminary, Judson and his first bride, Ann Hasseltine, sailed for India in 1812 as Congregational missionaries. They soon moved on to Burma (now Myanmar) where he suffered smallpox, tropical fevers, and nearly two years of brutal imprisonment. Ann endured terrible deprivations of her own, resulting in her death at the age of 36. Ann's own translation work and her heartrending stories of the sufferings of Burmese women found an eager audience in missionary magazines back home.

After Ann's death Judson married Sarah Hall Boardman, who worked with him shoulder to shoulder, spreading the gospel in the dangerous interior of Burma. Sarah completed the first translation of the New Testament into the Burmese language. When ill health claimed her life at the age of 42, Judson returned home for the first time in three decades and engaged a young writer named Emily Chubbuck to write Sarah's biography. They soon married and returned to Burma, where Judson himself died shortly afterward. By then he had completed monumental translation work and established a Burmese church with 7,000 followers. Emily's own illnesses and deprivations abroad resulted in her death from tuberculosis at the age of 36.

These tales became the stuff of legends. Were missionaries like the Judsons heroes? The answer is yes if measured by the popular acclaim they enjoyed at home. Many graduated from the best colleges, Presidents spoke at their conventions, and their missionary exploits captured front page coverage in secular and quasi-secular magazines like the *Christian Herald*.

At the same time, however, thoughtful men and women—including novelists Herman Melville and Mark Twain—argued that missionaries were more interested in spreading American civilization than Christianity. After all, Christian expansion often paralleled U.S. business and military development overseas. And some critics raised deeper, more troubling questions. Did missionaries have the right to displace other people's religions at all? Some missionaries lost their zeal in the face of such questions, but most carried on, convinced that they possessed a message to share. Though these determined evangelists hardly silenced their critics, most Americans ranked them among the most courageous of the religious adventurers of the 19th century.

Epilogue

At the end of the 20th century, religion in the United States seemed to hold more questions than answers. If visitors from a distant country had arrived in Washington, D.C., toured the Supreme Court and seen a session of Congress, then observed the classical Greek marble buildings lining the streets, they probably would have gained an impression that the United States was a wholly secular nation, without any references to God in its public life.

If they had ventured on to observe the immense, brooding statue of President Lincoln at the temple-like Lincoln Memorial, or the eternal flame burning at the tomb of President Kennedy, they might have suspected that Americans venerated their dead leaders very much as the ancient Romans had done—but they would not have sensed much else in the way of religion.

And if the travelers had journeyed northward to New York City, visited a board meeting at a Wall Street investment firm, or heard talk about maximizing profits, they might well have concluded that venerable notions about the divine ordering of human affairs had been lost somewhere along the way. A visit to the strip joints and seedy bars ringing any number of American towns and cities might have suggested that Americans were busy rebelling against the strict morals of their evangelical past in a headlong pursuit of immediate pleasure.

In this 1845 print, nine men of different Christian denominations gather around a Bible. The Native American (left) and the African American (right) in the background, reaching toward the light of the Holy Spirit, as well as the lion and lamb and the broken weapons in the foreground, suggest that the Christian faiths are uniting to convert others without strife.

On the other hand, if the visitors' plane had landed in Cincinnati, they would have encountered richly ornamented, well-attended synagogues of great beauty. A trip northward to Milwaukee would have afforded a skyline filled with the soaring steeples of Lutheran, Catholic, and Orthodox churches. Heading back south, they would have discovered countless Baptist meetinghouses marking the crossroads of just as many country roads. Moving west toward Salt Lake City the visitors would have seen Mormon assembly halls jammed with well-scrubbed worshipers. Los Angeles in turn would have presented a spectacle of Pentecostal megachurches, gleaming of glass and steel, complemented by an ever-growing number of Buddhist temples tucked away on palm-lined streets.

All this is to say that visitors might well have come away scratching their heads. Which was the real America? The one that seemed entirely secular? Or the one that glowed with treasured memories and sacred symbols? Clearly, one could make a case for either or both, depending on the time of day one looked. Americans, like most humans, tended to busy themselves with the ordinary affairs of life in the high noon of day, and seek the solace of faith in the lonely hours of night.

In all these respects the late 20th century was not so different from the late 19th or, for that matter, the late 18th century. The plain truth is that in the 19th century, religion did not occupy the attention of men and women all the time. Then as now Americans were deeply concerned with the challenges of making a living, rearing their children, getting along with their neighbors, and pursuing the simple (and sometimes not so simple) pleasures of life. But they also reflected on the meaning of their lives together. So they marked the passage of time with symbols and ceremonies. They set apart holy sites for the worship of God. They measured their days by ethical standards derived from ancient scriptures and time-honored traditions. And through prayer they tried to make the fragile, flickering candle of life burn a bit longer. To be sure, 19th-century religion bore its own distinctive features. But viewed from afar it represented a single episode in a long drama of human aspiration, played out on the vast stage of the North American continent.

Chronology

1730–40
The Great Awakening—revivals throughout the colonies propelled by the preaching of British evangelist George Whitefield

1731
First Masonic lodge in the colonies opened in Philadelphia (many of the founding fathers were Masons, including George Washington)

1771
Francis Asbury, later America's first Methodist bishop, volunteers for service in the colonies

1784
Methodist Episcopal Church founded. Hannah Adams, America's first professional woman writer, publishes the *Dictionary of All Religions*

1789
Church of England reorganizes as Protestant Episcopal Church in the United States

1790–1830
Second Great Awakening—a second major wave of religious revivals—begins in Kentucky and in Connecticut

1791
First Amendment ratified, including the phrase "Congress shall make no law respecting an establishment of religion, or prohibiting the free exercise thereof."

1800–1860
Number of African Americans swells from 1 million to 4 million—90 percent of whom live in southern slavery

1800
Congregationalists dominate, then Presbyterians and Baptists

1801
Outdoor camp meeting at Cane Ridge, Kentucky, attracts thousands

1809
Elizabeth Bayley Seton establishes Sisters of Charity in Baltimore, Maryland

1810
American Board of Commissioners for Foreign Missions organized

1816
African Methodist Episcopal Church founded in Philadelphia. American Bible Society formed from 100 independent Bible agencies

1819
American Colonization Society organized. Congregational missionaries from New England leave for Sandwich Islands (Hawaii)

1820s
German-speaking Jews begin arriving in the United States in large numbers

1821
African Methodist Episcopal Zion Church founded in New York. Charles Grandison Finney converted, leaves law practice to begin career as revivalist

1822
Denmark Vesey leads slave uprising in Charleston, South Carolina

1824
American Sunday School Union organized

1826
Society for the Promotion of Temperance organized

1830s
Stoneites and Campbellites form Christians/Disciples of Christ. Evangelicals in South largely cease to challenge the institution of slavery. Andrew Jackson marches Cherokees along the Trail of Tears to the Oklahoma Territory

1830s–1844
William Miller (forerunner of Seventh-day Adventists) preaches imminent return of Christ, dating the event first to March 21, 1843, then October 22, 1844

1830
Joseph Smith publishes *Book of Mormon*

1831
Nat Turner leads uprising in Southampton County, Virginia. William Lloyd Garrison launches abolitionist newspaper *The Liberator*

1832
"America" written by Baptist pastor Samuel F. Smith

1833
Massachusetts removes compulsory tax support for churches, last state to do so

1835, 1836
Anti-Catholic tracts "Six Months in a Convent" and "Awful Disclosures of the Hotel Dieu Nunnery of Montreal" published

1836
American Temperance Union formed

1837
Abolitionist editor Elijah P. Lovejoy murdered by a mob in Alton, Ill. Presbyterians split into Old School and New School

1837–1870s
Phoebe Palmer spreads the holiness message through her Tuesday Meetings for the Promotion of Christian Holiness and *Guide to Holiness*

1838
Ralph Waldo Emerson gives address at Harvard Divinity School, marking the beginnings of Romanticism and Transcendentalism in America

1841
John Humphrey Noyes founds Perfectionist commune in Vermont, which moved to Oneida, N.Y., in 1848

1844
Joseph Smith murdered. Methodists split over slavery

1845

Baptists split over slavery, Southern Baptist Convention formed

1846

Methodist circuit rider Peter Cartwright unsuccessfully runs for Congress against Abraham Lincoln. American Missionary Association formed to focus on educating freed slaves

1847

Mormons begin migrating to Utah Territory

1850s

Baptists and Methodists (both evangelical sects) together claim 70 percent of all Protestants. Reform Judaism develops under leadership of Isaac Mayer Wise. California gold rush—immigration of Asian laborers brings Eastern religions to West Coast

1852

Harriet Beecher Stowe publishes *Uncle Tom's Cabin*

1854

The anti-Catholic Know-Nothing party sends 75 men to Congress

1859

Charles Darwin publishes *Origin of The Species by Means of Natural Selection.* John Brown captures federal arsenal in Harpers Ferry, (West) Virginia, then is apprehended and hanged

1861

"Battle Hymn of the Republic" written by Unitarian activist Julia Ward Howe. Civil War begins

1865

Abraham Lincoln assassinated in Ford's Theater, Washington, D.C. Civil War ends; Thirteenth Amendment abolishes slavery

1870s–1890

Dwight L. Moody's evangelistic ministry gains large audiences in the northern and midwestern U.S. and Britain

1870–1910

Lutherans grow from one-half million to 2 million, largely by immigration, making them the fourth-largest denomination in the United States

1872

Russian Orthodox headquarters moved from Sitka, Alaska, to San Francisco

1875

Rabbi Isaac Mayer Wise founds Hebrew Union College in Cincinnati

1880s

Rise of "faith missions" such as the Africa Inland Mission and Sudan Interior Mission

1880s–90s

Buddhist missionaries visit Hawaiian Islands, then West Coast

1880s–1900s

Frances Willard leads nationwide crusade against alcohol, heads Woman's Christian Temperance Union

1880

Salvation Army arrives in the United States

1881

Mary Baker Eddy founds the Massachusetts Metaphysical College, the basis of the Church of Christ, Scientist (Christian Science).

1881–WORLD WAR I

23 million immigrants arrive in the United States

1884

Zion's Watch Tower Society (Jehovah's Witnesses) organized

1886

Dwight L. Moody founds the Student Volunteer Movement (SVM)

1890

Massacre of two hundred Sioux at Wounded Knee, South Dakota

1893

Heresy trial of Charles A. Briggs for teaching biblical higher criticism at Union Theological Seminary in New York

World's Parliament of Religions convened at the World's Columbian Exposition (popularly known as the World's Fair) in Chicago

1895

National Baptist Convention founded in Atlanta, Georgia

1897

Congregational minister Charles M. Sheldon publishes *In His Steps,* challenging Christians to ask in every situation "What would Jesus do?"

1899

Buddhist Churches of America formed

Pope Leo XIII issues encyclical warning against overaccommodation to American ways, called the Americanist controversy

1900

Catholics dominate, then Baptists and Methodists come to forefront

1901

Pentecostal movement begins, emphasizing divine healing and speaking in tongues

1908

Roman Catholic Church in the United States recognized by Rome as an autonomous national church rather than a "mission" run from Rome

Further Reading

GENERAL

Ahlstrom, Sydney E. *A Religious History of the American People.* New Haven, Conn.: Yale University Press, 1972.

Butler, Jon, and Harry S. Stout, eds. *Religion in American History: A Reader.* New York: Oxford University Press, 1997.

Gaustad, Edwin S. *A Religious History of America.* Revised edition. San Francisco: Harper & Row, 1990.

Marty, Martin. *Pilgrims in Their Own Land: 500 Years of Religion in America.* New York: Penguin, 1985.

RELIGION IN THE 19TH CENTURY

Arrington, Leonard J., et al. *Building the City of God: Community and Cooperation Among the Mormons.* 2nd ed. Urbana: University of Illinois Press, 1992.

Brereton, Virginia. *From Sin to Salvation: Stories of Women's Conversions, 1800 to the Present.* Bloomington: Indiana University Press, 1990.

Bull, Malcolm, and K. Lockhart. *Seeking a Sanctuary: Seventh-day Adventism and the American Dream.* San Francisco: Harper & Row, 1989.

Christiano, Kevin J. *Religious Diversity and Social Change: American Cities, 1890–1906.* New York: Cambridge University Press, 1987.

Curry, Thomas J. *The First Freedoms: Church and State in America to the Passage of the First Amendment.* New York: Oxford University Press, 1986.

Ellwood, Robert S., and Harry Partin. *Religious and Spiritual Groups in Modern America.* Englewood Cliffs, N.J.: Prentice-Hall, 1988.

Fields, Rick. *How the Swans Came to the Lake: A Narrative History of Buddhism in America.* 3d ed., rev. Boston: Shambhala, 1992.

Fogarty, Robert S. *All Things New: American Communes and Utopian Movements, 1860–1914*. Chicago: University of Chicago Press, 1990.

Gottschalk, Stephen. *The Emergence of Christian Science in American Religious Life*. Berkeley: University of California Press, 1973.

Humez, Jean M., ed. *Mother's First-Born Daughters: Early Shaker Writings on Women and Religion*. Bloomington: Indiana University Press, 1993.

Jessee, Dean C., ed. *The Personal Writings of Joseph Smith*. Salt Lake City, Utah: Deseret Book Co., 1984.

McDannell, Colleen. *The Christian Home in Victorian America, 1840–1900*. Bloomington: Indiana University Press, 1986.

Madsen, Carol C. *In Their Own Words: Women and the Story of Nauvoo*. Salt Lake City, Utah: Deseret Book Co., 1994.

Numbers, Ronald, and Jon Butler, eds. *The Disappointed: Miller and Millennarianism in the Nineteenth Century*. 2nd ed. Knoxville: University of Tennessee Press, 1987.

Stowe, Harriet Beecher. *Uncle Tom's Cabin*. 1852. Reprint, New York: Penguin, 1981.

Tarasar, Constance J., ed. *Orthodox America, 1794–1976*. Syosset, N.Y.: Orthodox Church in America, 1975.

Tweed, Thomas. *The American Encounter with Buddhism, 1844–1912*. Bloomington: Indiana University Press, 1992.

Wilson, John F. "Religion, Government, and Power in the New American Nation," in *Religion and American Politics from the Colonial Period to the 1980s*. Edited by Mark Noll. New York: Oxford University Press, 1990.

RELIGIOUS IDEAS

Adams, Dickinson W., ed. *Jefferson's Extracts from the Gospels*. Princeton, N.J.: Princeton University Press, 1983.

Adams, Hannah. *A Dictionary of All Religions and Religious Denominations*. 1817. Reprint, Atlanta: Scholars Press, 1992.

Livingstone, David N. *Darwin's Forgotten Defenders: The Encounter Between*

Evangelical Theology and Evolutionary Thought. Grand Rapids, Mich.: Eerdmans, 1987.

Moore, James R. *The Post-Darwinian Controversies: A Study of the Protestant Struggle to Come to Terms with Darwin in Great Britain and America, 1870–1900*. New York: Cambridge University Press, 1979.

Seager, Richard Hughes. *The Dawn of Religious Pluralism: Voices from the World's Parliament of Religions, 1893*. LaSalle, Ill.: Open Court, 1993.

Turner, James. *Without God, Without Creed: The Origins of Unbelief in America*. Baltimore: Johns Hopkins University Press, 1985.

RELIGION IN THE CIVIL WAR

Cherry, Conrad, ed. "Civil War and National Destiny," in *God's New Israel*. Revised edition. Chapel Hill: University of North Carolina, 1999.

Goen, C. C. *Broken Churches, Broken Nation: Denominational Schisms and the Coming of the American Civil War*. Macon, Ga.: Mercer University Press, 1985.

Jones, J. William. *Christ in the Camp or Religion in the Confederate Army, 1887*. Harrisonburg, Va.: Sprinkle Publications, 1986.

Shattuck, Gardiner H. *A Shield and Hiding Place: The Religious Life of the Civil War Armies*. Macon, Ga.: Mercer University Press, 1987.

AFRICAN AMERICANS

Andrews, William L. *Sisters of the Spirit: Three Black Women's Autobiographies of the Nineteenth Century*. Bloomington: Indiana University Press, 1986.

Harding, Vincent. "Religion and Resistance Among Antebellum Negroes, 1800–1860," in *The Making of Black America*, eds. August Meier and Elliot Rudwick. New York: Atheneum, 1969.

Raboteau, Albert. *Slave Religion: The "Invisible Institution" in the Antebellum South*. New York: Oxford University Press, 1978.

Sernett, William. *African American Religious History: A Documentary Witness*. Durham, N.C.: Duke University Press, 1989.

CATHOLICS

Abrahamson, Harold J. *Ethnic Diversity in Catholic America.* New York: Wiley, 1973.

Dolan, Jay P. *The Immigrant Church: New York's Irish and German Catholics, 1815–1865.* Baltimore: Johns Hopkins University Press, 1975.

Ellis, John T., ed. *Documents of American Catholic History.* Revised edition. Chicago: H. Regnery, 1967.

JEWS

Blau, Joseph. *Judaism in America.* Chicago: University of Chicago Press, 1976.

Blau, Joseph, and Salo W. Baron. *The Jews of the United States, 1790–1840: A Documentary History.* New York: Columbia University Press, 1966.

Dinnerstein, Leonard. *Anti-Semitism in America.* New York: Oxford University Press, 1994.

Karp, Abraham J., ed. *The Jewish Experience in America: Documentary History.* 5 vols. Waltham, Mass.: American Jewish Historical Society, 1969.

Kraut, Benny. *From Reform Judaism to Ethical Culture: The Religious Evolution of Felix Adler.* Cincinnati: Hebrew Union College Press, 1979.

NATIVE AMERICANS

Bowden, Henry W. *American Indians and Christian Missions.* Chicago: University of Chicago Press, 1981.

Capps, Walter H., ed. *Seeing with a Native Eye.* New York: Harper & Row, 1976.

Hultkrantz, Ake. *The Religions of the American Indians.* Berkeley: University of California Press, 1979.

McLoughlin, William G. *The Cherokees and Christianity: 1794–1870.* Athens: University of Georgia Press, 1994.

PROTESTANTS

Abell, Aaron I. *The Urban Impact on American Protestantism, 1865–1900.* Cambridge: Harvard University Press, 1943.

Boles, John. *The Great Revival: 1787–1805.* Revised edition. Lexington: University Press of Kentucky, 1996.

Brereton, Virginia. *Training God's Army: The American Bible School, 1880–1940.* Bloomington: Indiana University Press, 1990.

Boylan, Anne M. *Sunday School: The Formation of an American Institution, 1790–1880.* New Haven: Yale University Press, 1988.

Carpenter, Joel A., and Wilbert R. Shenk, eds. *Earthen Vessels: American Evangelicals and Foreign Missions, 1880–1980.* Grand Rapids, Mich.: Eerdmans, 1990.

Conkin, Paul K. *Cane Ridge: America's Pentecost.* Madison: University of Wisconsin Press, 1990.

Curtis, Susan. *A Consuming Faith: The Social Gospel and Modern American Culture.* Baltimore: Johns Hopkins University Press, 1991.

Findlay, James F. *Dwight L. Moody: American Evangelist, 1837–1899.* Chicago: University of Chicago Press, 1969.

Finney, Charles G. *Lectures on Revivals in Religion.* Edited by William G. McLoughlin. Cambridge: Harvard University Press, 1960.

Garrett, Leroy. *The Stone-Campbell Movement: An Anecdotal History of Three Churches.* Joplin, Mo.: College Press, 1981.

Griffin, Clifford S. *Their Brothers' Keepers: Moral Stewardship in the United States, 1800–1865.* New Brunswick, N.J.: Rutgers University Press, 1960.

Heyrman, Christine Leigh. *Southern Cross: The Beginnings of the Bible Belt.* New York: Knopf, 1997.

Hutchison, William R. *Errand to the World: American Protestant Thought and Foreign Missions.* Chicago: University of Chicago Press, 1987.

Jones, Charles E. *Perfectionist Persuasion: The Holiness Movement and American Methodism, 1867–1936.* Metuchen, N.J.: Scarecrow, 1974.

McLoughlin, William G., ed. *The American Evangelicals, 1800–1900: An Anthology.* New York: Harper & Row, 1968.

Magnuson, Norris. *Salvation in the Slums: Evangelical Social Work, 1865–1920.* Grand Rapids, Mich.: Baker Book House, 1990.

Marsden, George. *Fundamentalism and American Culture: The Shaping of Twentieth Century Evangelicalism, 1870–1925.* New York: Oxford University Press, 1980.

Mathews, Donald G. *Religion in the Old South.* Chicago: University of Chicago Press, 1977.

Murdoch, Norman H. *Origins of the Salvation Army.* Knoxville: University of Tennessee Press, 1994.

Oden, Thomas C., ed. *Phoebe Palmer: Selected Writings.* New York: Paulist Press, 1988.

Powell, Milton B., ed. *The Voluntary Church: American Religious Life, 1740–1860, Seen Through the Eyes of European Visitors.* New York: Macmillan, 1967.

Semmel, Bernard. *The Methodist Revolution.* New York: Basic Books, 1973.

Sizer, Sandra. *Gospel Hymns and Social Religion.* Philadelphia: Temple University Press, 1978.

Synan, Vinson. *The Holiness-Pentecostal Movement in America.* Grand Rapids, Mich.: Eerdmans, 1971.

Weber, Timothy P. *Living in the Shadow of the Second Coming: American Premillennialism, 1875–1925.* Chicago: University of Chicago Press, 1987.

Wright, Conrad, ed. *Three Prophets of Religious Liberalism: Channing, Emerson, Parker.* Boston: Beacon, 1961.

Acknowledgments

A variety of sources have informed this book. Although many are listed in the Further Reading section, I am particularly indebted to four surveys of American religion for data, quotations, and helping me think about the overall structure of the narrative. These include Catherine L. Albanese, *America: Religions and Religion* (Belmont, Calif.: Wadsworth, 1992, 2nd ed.); Mark A. Noll, *A History of Christianity in the United States and Canada* (Grand Rapids, Mich.: Eerdmans, 1992); Peter W. Williams, *America's Religions: Traditions and Cultures* (New York: Macmillan, 1990); and *Eerdmans' Handbook to Christianity in America,* edited by David F. Wells and others (Grand Rapids, Mich.: Eerdmans, 1983), especially the section on the 19th century by Nathan O. Hatch and sidebar authors Stephen E. Berk, James E. Johnson, John B. Boles, Howard A. Snyder, Sandra S. Sizer, Ronald L. Numbers, Lawrence Foster, Donald E. Pitzer, Wesley A. Roberts, Thomas A. Askew, Rockne McCarthy, Joseph M. White, Patrick Carey, Michael J. Roach, Thomas J. Schlereth, Jay P. Dolan, Ronald A. Wells, Ronald D. Rietveld, Donald Tinder, Susan B. Hoekema, Norris Magnuson, Anthony A. Hoekema, James W. Skillen, C. Norman Kraus, and David B. Wills.

James H. Hutson, *Religion and the Founding of the American Republic* (Hanover, N.H.: University Press of New England, 1998), provided valuable information on the founding generation. Two handbooks merit particular credit: *Dictionary of Christianity in America,* edited by Daniel G. Reid and others (Downers Grove, Ill.: InterVarsity Press, 1990), and Henry Warner Bowden, *Dictionary of American Religious Biography* (Westport, Conn.: Greenwood, 1977). The Sound Editions audiotape *The Civil War,* by Geoffrey C. Ward with Ric Burns and Ken Burns, supplied important ideas and choice details. Other particularly helpful works included Ronald L. Numbers, *Prophetess of Health: Ellen G. White and the Origins of Seventh-day Adventism Health Reform* (Knoxville: University of Tennessee Press, 1992), Catherine L. Albanese, *Sons of the Fathers: The Civil Religion of the American Revolution* (Philadelphia: Temple University Press, 1976), Nell Irvin Painter, *Sojourner Truth: A Life, A Symbol* (New York: W.W. Norton, 1996), and David Gollaher, *Voice for the Mad: The Life of Dorothea Dix* (New York: Free Press, 1995). R. Laurence Moore, "What Children Did Not Learn in School: The Intellectual Quickening of Young Americans in the Nineteenth Century," *Church History* 68 (March 1999) 42–61, provided ideas about Elizabeth Cady Stanton. Chapter 8, "Innovators," contained several sentences from my essay, "A Plural World: The Protestant Awakening to World Religions," in *Between the Times: The Travail of the Protestant Establishment, 1900–1960,* edited by William R. Hutchison (New York: Cambridge University Press, 1989).

Numerous individuals have helped. Chris Armstrong, Joanne Beckman, Russ Congleton, and Susie Mroz, all doctoral students in American religious history at Duke University, labored diligently to spot errors and simplify obscure prose. Rosalee Velloso de Silva corrected the bibliography. Julie Byrne provided data on Roman Catholics. I especially wish to thank Professors William R. Hutchison, Robert Bruce Mullin, and Harry S. Stout, as well as Oxford University Press editorial director Nancy Toff and managing editor Katherine Adzima, who offered valuable criticisms of early drafts of the manuscript.

Picture Credits

Text Credits

FOR CHAPTER EPIGRAPHS:
Chapters 1–3, 6–10: *The United Methodist Hymnal: Book of United Methodist Worship* (Nashville, Tenn.: United Methodist Publishing House, 1989).

Chapter 4: *The Hymnal: Reorganized Church of Jesus Christ of Latter Day Saints* (Independence, Mo.: Herald Publishing House, 1956).

Chapter 5: *The Cokesbury Worship Hymnal,* C. A. Bowen, ed. (New York: Abingdon-Cokesbury Press, n.d.).

FOR TEXTS QUOTED IN CHAPTERS:
Chapter 1: St. Jean de Crevecoeur, J. Hector. *Letters from an American Farmer* (1782), excerpted in *New World Metaphysics: Religious Readings on the Religious Meaning of the American Experience,* edited by Giles Gunn (New York: Oxford University Press, 1981), 134.

Chapter 2: Woodward, William W., ed. *Surprising Accounts of the Revival of Religion in the United States of America...* (1802), excerpted in *American Christianity: An Historical Interpretation with Representative Documents,* 2 vols., edited by H. Shelton Smith, et. al. (New York: Charles Scribner's Sons, 1960), I:568.

Chapter 7: Cather, Willa. *Death Comes for the Archbishop* (1927) (New York: Random House, 1990), 81.

SIDEBARS:
"Thomas Jefferson Writes of the Freedom to Choose," p. 17: Giles Gunn, ed., *New World Metaphysics: Religious Readings on the Religious Meaning of the American Experience* (New York: Oxford University Press, 1981), 129–31.

"A Memorable Call to the Ministry," p. 38: Charles G. Finney, *An Autobiography* (Old Tappan, N. J.: Fleming H. Revell Company, 1908), 20–21.

"Phoebe Palmer's Religious Feminism," p. 145: Phoebe Palmer, *Promise of the Father* (New York: Garland, 1985), 329–30, 333–34.

"God's Messenger Moroni Visits Joseph Smith," p. 67: Joseph Smith, *The History of Joseph Smith, by Himself* (1838), excerpted in "Religion and Cultural Change in American History," edited by William R. Hutchison (readings for NEH Summer Seminar, 1986, Harvard University), n.p.

"Rabbi Wise Speaks of the Wisdom of Change," p. 83: I. M. Wise, *Selected Writings* (1900), excerpted in *A Documentary History of Religion in America: Since 1865,* edited by Edwin S. Gaustad (Grand Rapids, Mich.: Eerdmans Publishing, 1983), 55–6.

"Christianity and the Slaveholding Religion," p. 100: Giles Gunn, ed., *New World Metaphysics: Religious Readings on the Religious Meaning of the American Experience* (New York: Oxford University Press, 1981), 192–93.

"A Nun's Letter to Germany," p. 113: Rosemary Radford Ruether and Rosemary Skinner Keller, eds., *Women and Religion in America,* 3 vols. (San Francisco: Harper & Row, 1981), II:126.

"Mary Baker Eddy Stresses Mind Over Matter," p. 158: excerpted in "Religion and Cultural Change in American History," edited by William R. Hutchison (readings for NEH Summer Seminar, 1986, Harvard University), n.p.

"Father Pierre Jean De Smet's Work with the Sioux," p. 50: *Life, Letters, and Travels of Father De Smet* (1904), excerpted in *A Documentary History of Religion in America: Since 1865,* edited by Edwin S. Gaustad (Grand Rapids, Mich.: Eerdmans Publishing, 1983), 72–5.

Grant Wacker

Grant Wacker is associate professor of the history of religion in America at the Divinity School of Duke University. He has written articles on the liberal, the evangelical, and the Pentecostal traditions in America, and is a senior editor of the quarterly journal *Church History: Studies in Christianity and Culture.*

Jon Butler

Jon Butler is the William Robertson Coe Professor of American Studies and History and Professor of Religious Studies at Yale University. He received his B.A. and Ph.D. in history from the University of Minnesota. He is the coauthor, with Harry S. Stout, of *Religion in American History: A Reader,* and the author of several other books in American religious history including *Awash in a Sea of Faith: Christianizing the American People,* which won the Beveridge Award for the best book in American history in 1990 from the American Historical Association.

Harry S. Stout

Harry S. Stout is the Jonathan Edwards Professor of American Christianity at Yale University. He is the general editor of the Religion in America series for Oxford University Press and co-editor of *Readings in American Religious History, New Directions in American Religious History, A Jonathan Edwards Reader,* and *The Dictionary of Christianity in America.* His book *The Divine Dramatist: George Whitefield and the Rise of Modern Evangelicalism* was nominated for a Pulitzer Prize in 1991.